CONTENTS

INTRODUCTION	8
CHAPTER 1 : My Humble Beginnings	11
CHAPTER 2: The Journey	21
CHAPTER 3: Life In Abeokuta 1989 -1999	33
CHAPTER 4: Becoming Mrs. Nwaefuna	39
CHAPTER 5: Dream Takes Flight	44
CHAPTER 6: Navigating AMerica	50
CHAPTER 7: A Joyful Reunion/A New Chapter Begins	61
CHAPTER 8: My Education and Career Journey	69
CHAPTER 9: My Philanthropic Mission	83
CHAPTER 10: The Emergence of a Star Baby	90
EPILOGUE	104

Dear Reader,

Life is a journey, full of ups and downs but discovering the real you is a footing to Rebranding your destiny —
—— shalom!   Dr. Patricia Nwaefung
5/18/24

DR. PATRICIANWAEFUNA

Rebranded By Grace: Then And Now

My Personal Life Journey: A Narrative

This is an inspiring true story of a Nigerian-American woman who overcame significant obstacles to attain success.

Dedication

To the Sovereign Lord:

This chronicle of my life, laced with drift of struggle, sorrow, triumph, and joy, I humbly lay at your feet most Sovereign Lord. Your absolute rulership over me, protecting me from Earthly shadows and guiding me towards my predestined purpose, is undeniable. You are the Potter who shaped my clay, the Discoverer who revealed my path, the Defender who shielded me from harm, and the Sustainer who carried me through every storm.

Thank you Lord, for the strength you infuse into feeble hearts like mine. For being my refuge in times of need, my resource when all else fails. You are indeed the way maker, miracle worker, destiny changer, the promise keeper. You are the unwavering anchor in the tempestuous sea of life. My trust, my complete dependence on you, has woven its resilient threads into the fabric of my being. Your grace and mercy have seen me through valleys I could not conquer alone. Without your sovereign hand upon me, I would be lost.

You transformed me from a self-willed soul to a vessel filled with light, proving the truth of your words in Romans 9:15: "I will have mercy on whom I will have mercy, and compassion on whom I will have compassion." Through your divine compassion, I found release from physical, mental, and emotional burdens, and was repositioned for a life bathed in peace and love. This is my story, a testament to your steady love, a hymn sung to your everlasting grace. May it serve as a beacon of hope for all who seek your hand in life's uncertainties.

With unfaltering devotion,

Your daughter, Patricia Nwaefuna.

ACKNOWLEDGMENT

With a bow of gratitude, I humble myself to honor the Person of the Holy Spirit for His continued presence in my life. He has been my constant companion on this journey. My partner, coach, motivator, director, and therapist. Your gentleness is calming, and your expert knowledge is informing. Thank you for your counsel, wisdom, and fortitude to pen this memoir. Your unwavering light led the way throughout this project. I am forever indebted.

Honoring My Husband:

My deepest thanks flow to my cherished husband, Mr. Victor Ndubisi Nwaefuna - my soulmate, prince charming, and dearest friend. You have willingly and lovingly walked beside me on this path. You are the wind beneath my wings, the steady pillar by my side. You are the leading character in the grand tapestry of my life. I bless the day you graced the world and the womb that nurtured you. You are an answered prayer, and this story would be incomplete without your partnership. God's hand in bringing you into my life is something I cherish every day. You saw my flaws and all, and embraced me nonetheless. Truly, you are a rare gem, a gift not just to me but to the world itself. A million thanks, my love, together we shall reach a glorious ending, Amen.

To My Precious Diamonds:

Laura, Bernice, Aaron, Nathan, and Lael Nwaefuna - you are the reason my heart beats a little faster, the stars that guide me through the darkness. Because of you, I rise each morning with renewed purpose, knowing the future holds treasures laced with our shared laughter and love. You are anointed to blossom, each a unique spark destined to set the world alight. Remember, no matter where life's winds may carry you, my love will always be your anchor.

My Sibling Constellation:

Ambassador Chief Solomon Umoke, Hon. Elizabeth Nwaenyi, Mrs. Angelina Obasi, Mr. Sunday Umoke, Rev Dr. Elijah Umoke, and Barrister Jacob Umoke, you are the memories of my roots, netted with laughter and shared experiences. Thank you for the steadfast support, the gentle nudges when I faltered, and the infectious laughter that chased away doubt. Chief Solomon, your vision and selflessness reshaped my path, proving that new life can bloom from unexpected branches.

Angels in Human Form:

I extend my heartfelt thanks to my brother-in-law, Dr. Hypsy Nwaefuna, for his unwavering support during a challenging time. Your presence when I needed it most was truly invaluable. May God answer your prayers in return, as I pray in the mighty name of Jesus.

My deepest gratitude goes to Mrs. Rosemary Menye for her incredible hospitality. You opened your home to me upon my arrival in the United States, demonstrating a heart of pure gold.

To my godparents, Pastors Wale and Kemi Arogundade, I express my sincere appreciation for your love, care, and generosity. Your genuine kindness is a rare treasure. You embraced me during a time of despair, offering a comforting shoulder to lean on. Your actions truly reflect your teachings.

To Pastors Lanre and Abiola Peters, you are embodiment of love and wisdom. Your exceptional leadership and exemplary character inspires me greatly. I thank God for allowing our parts to cross. Your tireless prayers and encouragement made a lasting difference; and your unwavering support were whispers of hope in the quiet hours.

I extend my gratitude to Dr. Temilayo Owusu-Addo and Mr. Dodji Koudakpo for their tireless support, and for reviewing this book for accuracy, and for offering constructive feedback.

To all my church family members and friends whose paths have crossed mine by God's design. Each of you holds a special place in my heart, and your unique presence is deeply appreciated.

To Dr. Adebukola Abiola, your wisdom and mentorship nurtured my dreams, and your friendship a guiding light on my path.

A Beacon of Inspiration:

Oprah Winfrey, your life story is a testament to resilience; your voice a clarion call to embrace audacious dreams. You remind us that the past, though etched in our hearts, should not define our future. Thank you for showing us the way.

INTRODUCTION

Unlike the journey of countless others, my story is unique in its details yet universal in its spirit. It is a testament to resilience, a chronicle of finding strength in the face of adversity and carving one's own path through the unyielding road of life. It is a story that yearns to be told, for within its pages lie the echoes of my own struggles and triumphs and the seeds of inspiration for generations to come.

So, gather close, dear readers and let me take you on a journey unlike any other. Let me show you the world through the eyes of a young lady who dared to dream beyond the confines of her village, who dared to chase the whispers of hope even when the path ahead seemed shrouded in darkness. This is my story, a celebration of the unyielding road that we all must travel, a testament to the radiant gold that can be woven from the humble dust of beginnings.

Everyone has a history and a story to tell, and I have tailored mine in this chronicle. In my journey so far on Earth, I have come to realize that when grace is induced into a person's life, destiny is sure; and grace to me is undeserved leniency, clemency, strength, and charity, and it's only available to those who willingly dethrone their self-efforts and accept God's help. If we trust in ourselves more than we trust in God, we can fall from grace. On that note I say to you that every situation has a scheduled solution, it's just a matter of time; and everyone has a destiny to fulfill, but grace makes the difference.

I have heard people talk about their background with a high level of rue, but our background symbolizes our foundation, roots, and connection. Life will lack meaning without a foundation as it empowers us to live and make life choices that are in alignment with our true identity. It helps to foster a sense of purpose and fulfillment. Nonetheless, our background does not necessarily determine what we become in life.

My story is born from the fertile ground of grace, not as a mere happenstance, but as a divine hand extended, offering undeserved favor, unyielding strength, and boundless love. It blooms only in the soil of surrender, where the tendrils of self-reliance wither and give way to an unshakeable trust in something greater.

For every stumble, there's a destined rise. Every tear, a whispered promise of joy. We all march to the beat of our own predestined drum, but it's the embrace of grace that sets the tempo, transforming life's melody from a hesitant hum to a triumphant symphony.

This journey you hold in your hands isn't just a testament to a transformative power, it's an invitation to step into the vibrant world of grace, where burdens are lifted, fears dissolved, and destinies unfolded like petals kissed by the sun. So, turn the page, dear readers, and let's dance together to the rhythm of divine favor, for within these pages lies not just my story, but a reflection of your own, waiting to be illuminated by the steady glow of grace.

My name is Patricia Nwafor Nwaefuna. Imagine coming through the sun-drenched fields of a remote Nigerian village, a path lined with whispers of ancient traditions and dappled with the shadows of cultural assumptions.

This is where my journey began, on June 6, 1974, in the embrace of a loving but impoverished family. I am a doctor of Nursing Practice, specializing in psychiatry. Beyond my clinical background, I wear many hats: mental health coach, philanthropist, wife, and a mother to five adorable children. Most importantly, a devoted child of God. My faith is the cornerstone of my life, characterized by a uniquely cherished daughter-father relationship with God.

I hail from a background of humble beginnings where female education was a rarity. Despite the prevailing social taboos, I persevered and became one of the first in my generation to achieve a doctoral degree in my chosen career field. This is an accomplishment that only God can confer, and stands as a testament to the unwavering spirit and the power of opportunity.

Fueled by a lifelong love for humanity, I've dedicated myself to making a positive impact on the lives of others. This passion led me to establish the "Grace upon Grace Foundation International" in Africa, specifically focusing on aiding the underprivileged and widows in Nigeria (detailed in subsequent chapter).

This is my invitation to you, dear readers, to join me on this extraordinary journey. Turn the page and let us navigate the labyrinthine paths of my life, from a dusty soil of humble beginnings to sun-drenched peaks of personal triumph. Witness the metamorphosis of a woman nurtured by tradition, defying limitations, and ultimately claiming her own destiny.

CHAPTER 1 : MY HUMBLE BEGINNINGS

In my experience, I have encountered individuals who held the belief that a person's socioeconomic background significantly impacts not only the career opportunities available to them, but also their overall life trajectory. Others believe that early childhood experiences often shape who we become, with lessons learned and values guiding our choices. However, are these always the case? Probably not; as there are many out there including myself whose background has nothing to do with what they became in life.

Another common belief holds that identity is the core aspect of every life, shaping our aspirations and guiding our destinies. However, I propose that self-discovery, the process of uncovering your authentic self, is the key to unlocking your true potential and reshaping your destiny. Self-discovery delves into the depths of your being, encompassing your ego, psyche, personality, and the unique essence of who you are. Lack of self identity and confidence often lead individuals to mimic the lives of others. Unsure of their own identities and capabilities, they risk losing touch with their true selves. This misalignment can breed feelings of inadequacy and incompetence.

I readily admit to once being lost in this very pattern. Disconnected from my core identity, I struggled to envision my potential. My worth seemed dependent on external validation, and I constantly felt pressured to conform to others' expectations. Past attempts to mirror seemingly successful individuals, their ambitions, confidence, their definition of enough, who appeared to have it all figured out, resulted in nothing but failure.

The journey of self-discovery was a long and winding road for me. Finally, after much introspection, I unearthed my true self. This revelation brought a profound understanding: there is no singular, predetermined purpose for life. My path diverged significantly from those I once emulated, and I came to realize that those lacking a strong sense of self often find themselves living according to the expectations of others.

Life unfolds in diverse ways. Some find fulfillment in the simple joy of everyday life, while others pursue grand ambitions. To successfully navigate your own path of self-discovery is paramount. And understanding your unique strengths, passions, and values is essential in identifying your life's purpose.

Speaking from personal experience, I want to assure both women and men that your background or birthplace does not dictate your destiny. While a guiding hand may exist, we each play an active role in shaping our futures. Embrace the journey of self-discovery, and unlock the potential to create the life you envision.

The challenges of life are an enduring presence, a constant thread woven through the tapestry of human experience, from our ancestors to generations yet to come. In our contemporary world, the focus has shifted from background as a sole determinant of success. While background isn't entirely irrelevant, self-discovery holds greater weight. It's through self-discovery that we build resilience within ourselves; a crucial tool for navigating life's inevitable challenges. This resilience serves as inner strength that sets us apart, empowering us to emerge victorious.

As I share my story, I downplay personal merit because life achievements often come at a cost – struggle, hard work, stress, and various challenges. Instead, I attribute my journey to the grace and inherent abilities bestowed upon me by God. This divine grace serves as the gateway to a life of faith and fulfillment.

Before the person I am today, I have experienced setbacks, misfortune, failures, and poverty first hand. These challenges were met with resilience and grace, a powerful combination that fostered positive adaptation within me.

I hail from a rural village in eastern Nigeria, a place where peasant farming formed the backbone of the community. Born into the family of the late Mr. Joseph and Deaconess Christiana Umoke, my arrival coincided with a famous market day known as "Afor." This auspicious occasion not only marked my entrance into the world but also determined my middle name. Named after my paternal great-grandmother, Nwafor, a tradition emerged – I became the living namesake.

I am the fifth and youngest daughter of eight biological children of my parents. For reasons unknown to me, my siblings held the playful belief that I was our father's favorite. Perhaps it stemmed from our resemblance – a shared physical stature and the honor of being named after his grandmother.

My story exemplifies God's overflowing grace, a quality not

only superior but also infinitely abundant. I speak to you as a vessel of divine grace and expression, created to fulfill a unique purpose on Earth.

My Father: A Man of Many Trades

My father was a multifaceted individual, skilled in several pursuits. He practiced hunting, peasant farming, and even blacksmithing. While none of these activities occupied him full-time, hunting held a special place in his heart. He spent a significant amount of time venturing deep into the bush, both day and night, tracking various animals. His keen observation skills allowed him to map their movements during the day, facilitating successful hunts under the cloak of darkness. The fruits of his labor provided for our family's protein needs. He hunted a wide variety of animals, including fish, birds, squirrels, rabbits, guinea fowls, and many more.

Blacksmithing was another of his talents. He crafted essential tools like hoes and cutlasses for the local farmers. Barter, rather than monetary exchange, fueled these transactions. Payment typically came in the form of yams, a staple food source for many families.

My Mother's Resourcefulness

My mother displayed remarkable resourcefulness as a petty trader. Operating on a retail scale, she bought and sold various goods, including yams and occasionally, soft drinks like Coca-Cola products. Neither of my parents had the privilege of formal education. Our family circumstances were marked by significant financial limitations. Providing two substantial meals a day was often a challenge. It's important to clarify that these meals wouldn't have included rice, beans, meat, fish, chicken, or milk – staples often associated with a more affluent lifestyle. Our typical fare consisted of *garri* or *fufu*, a cassava flour-based dish, accompanied by a locally prepared soup.

Hardship and Hope: A Mother's Story

My mother's recollections of my birth paint a picture of hardship and resilience. According to her narrative, our community was gripped by famine during her pregnancy with me. Food scarcity was severe, limiting her access to proper nourishment. The community well, a shared source of water for both villagers and livestock, run dry. Desperate for their families' survival, people embarked on arduous journeys on foot to neighboring villages, all in search of water.

My mother's diet for those nine months consisted primarily of palm kernel and cocoyam, a testament to her resourcefulness in the face of extreme limitations. Rainwater became her only source of hydration. She recounted how my underdeveloped physique upon arrival incited comparisons to a lizard, highlighting the impact of those challenging circumstances.

A Dramatic Entry into the World

My birth, my mother recalled, came not in sterile hospital walls but under the open sky, with her strength alone guiding me into the world. According to her tale, my delivery was a dramatic one. While in labor, she left the farm and moved closer to our house. With instincts taking hold, she birthed me on the ground. Following a brief moment, she retrieved an old razor blade from the house to sever the umbilical cord. Upon returning, she was startled to find a large snake approaching me. With a shout of "Jesus," she recounted that the snake changed course, slithering away in a different direction. Relieved, she wrapped me in her cloth and alerted my father of my birth. He then performed the traditional task of burying the cord and placenta in a designated location, adhering to the local custom, believed to ward off misfortune and associated ailments.

Childhood in a Bygone Era: Nutritional Realities

Modern nutritional wisdom emphasizes the importance of essential nutrients for a child's development. However, my childhood, unfolding in a historical period far removed from contemporary conveniences, differed greatly. As an infant, I was unable to breastfeed for the first three months of my life due to insufficient lactation. I relied on rainwater – a stark contrast to the recommended practices of today.

By the age of four months, the transition was made to solid food, specifically pounded yam, a staple food source in our community. This dietary shift reflected the limited availability of breast milk. As I transitioned into toddlerhood, the scarcity and expense of pounded yam necessitated a change. Henceforth, I shared meals with the rest of the family. On rare occasions, my father would secure a tuber of yam to supplement the family's diet, and on even luckier days, plantain porridge might grace our lunchtime table.

Life in a Remote Village: Resourcefulness and Tradition

Modern healthcare facilities were entirely absent from my village life. Hospitals, maternity homes, clinics, and pharmacies were distant realities. The villagers relied on traditional herbal remedies for various ailments, and my own childhood mirrored this experience.

Vivid memories surface of my mother venturing into the bush to gather herbs whenever sickness struck among my siblings and I. Leaves, bark, and roots would be carefully collected, combined in a pot, and boiled for hours to create a concentrated solution. This herbal concoction served as a treatment for common illnesses like malaria, typhoid fever, and constipation. Through consistent use and positive outcomes, my mother's skill in utilizing these traditional remedies earned her the reputation of the local "chemist" within our community.

It's important to note that my mother lacked formal education and medical training. Perhaps even more remarkable, she delivered all of her children, myself included, without the assistance of a midwife or healthcare provider. Her unwavering dedication to our family's well-being is further underscored by her tireless work on the farm. Year-round, she toiled under the harsh sun, ensuring a bountiful cassava harvest – a staple food source for our family. Throughout her pregnancies, she shouldered these responsibilities without assistance from my father or others.

A Childhood Steeped in Self-Reliance

My childhood instilled in me a sense of bravery, wisdom gleaned from my father, and a high-spirited nature. By the age of eight, I had learned to navigate the local markets, independently purchasing groceries like pepper and salt for my mother. Fear was a foreign concept those days; the danger of speeding cars, kidnappings, serial killers, or even bullies were absent realities in our community. My parents, recognizing the value of self-sufficiency, instilled vigilance and independence in all of us from a young age.

Driven by the hope of securing two meals a day for myself, I joined the local farmers' club for my age group at the age of ten. We were eight girls in total, united in our contribution to the family's agricultural efforts.

Our farmers' club fostered a spirit of shared adventure. Each week, we would rotate our efforts, dedicating a day to work on each other's family farms. This system ensured that all four member families received assistance over a one-week period. The cycle would then repeat, guaranteeing that each member benefited from collective labor. Our primary tasks involved weeding and harvesting ripe crops, contributing significantly to the families' agricultural output.

At that tender age, my responsibilities extended beyond the club. I diligently rose early each morning to fetch water for the family from the stream, ensuring our household needs were met. Maintaining a clean environment was also a priority, and I would meticulously sweep our compound. Following these chores, I would utilize a chewing stick for my morning oral hygiene before joining my club for the day's work.

Together we enjoyed the camaraderie of gathering firewood in the forest – our primary source of fuel for cooking.

My childhood existence differed vastly from the experiences of many children today. Rice, a staple food in many cultures, graced our table only once a year, during the Christmas season. The concept of childhood vaccinations, a cornerstone of modern healthcare, was entirely absent from my reality. While some kids today have perfect schedules, filled with vitamins and fancy baby food, my childhood was like an old story, happening before all the things we think we need now. My first bedtime songs were raindrops pattering on the roof, singing me to sleep. Yet, despite this spartan landscape, I thrived. No fever ravaged my small frame, no cavities marred my smile. What was this, if not grace?

My life wasn't all about hand-me-downs and empty cupboards, rather it can best be attributed to a sense of inherent grace that watched over me during my formative years. In those days, lessons bloomed beneath the sun, and responsibility tasted like sweet cassava after a day's work. Each challenge was a stepping stone, each sunrise a promise of adventure. My experience nurtured a wellspring of empathy, and the urge to spread kindness like wildflowers across the parched Earth. This is a testament to the power of grace, not as a lucky touch.

This story of mine is made from all the tough times, the happy laughter, and the rich Earth that filled my childhood with sunshine and the love of my whole village. You could call it the quiet magic of resilience and grace, etched in the lessons of a simple life. In my setbacks, God was my refuge;

in my misfortunes, He was a steady light. And so, I speak not as a lone conqueror, but as a vessel overflowing with divine grace. This is a testament to God's miraculous power that can sculpt purpose and meaning from even the most barren ground. A whisper of thanks to the unseen force that pulled me through the shadows into the light.

CHAPTER 2: THE JOURNEY

Grass isn't merely decorative; it holds symbolic meaning. Its presence speaks of roots, connection, and a foundation. Envision a landscape devoid of grass. Erosion, mudslides, and the ravages of weather would be inevitable. Grass, in this sense, is more than just a plant; it's a vital element, offering a silent lesson in stability and resilience.

However, the concept goes deeper. "Grass" and "grace" are words with a subtle difference. While a grassy field might symbolize emptiness, grace is a divine force that brings favor, protection, and a connection to the divine realm. It lifts us, propels us forward, and shelters us from storms. It draws us towards unexpected blessings; and when grace is bestowed upon an individual, it acts as a compass, guiding one's journey through life.

My life's journey is a path sculpted from the emerald threads of resilience and the golden whispers of grace. It's a story of stumbles and triumphs of lessons learned amidst the swaying fields of life. I invite you to join me on this exploration. Let's trace the roots that anchor us, feel the wind of grace upon our faces, and discover the path that beckons us onward.

To illustrate my point, let me turn to a figure from the Bible whose story resonates with my own. David, the youngest of eight brothers, was often overlooked. Considered insignificant in the affairs of his father's kingdom, and viewed as both young and of slight stature, he was primarily entrusted with tending to his father's livestock. Few would have predicted his ascent to the throne. However, when chosen by God (faith beamed upon him), his life took on a new significance. He became a pivotal figure, not only in his own time but to generations beyond.

Unlike humans who judge by outward appearances, God sees the heart. This is precisely why David, a humble shepherd, was chosen for greatness. Though David remained unknown in the wider world, his pure heart did not escape God's notice. Beneath his youthful exterior, beats a heart of loyalty and faith unseen by men, but radiant in God's eyes. It was this unseen quality, not broad shoulders or battlefield prowess, that drew the divine spotlight onto David.

The demonstration of God's favor in David's life was undeniable. With a simple sling and stone, he felled the formidable Goliath, a giant who had terrified the Israelites. This act propelled David from obscurity to a position of immense honor. He ascended to become the greatest king and leader in Israel's history, ushering in a golden age marked by significant achievements. During his reign, the Israelites flourished. He was credited with composing many of the Psalms, those beautiful expressions of faith that continue to resonate today.

David's legacy extends beyond his reign. He secured the threshing floor of Araunah, a seemingly ordinary purchase that held immense significance. It was this very site that King Solomon, David's son, built the magnificent first Temple. Significantly, David's lineage gave rise to Jesus Christ, our Savior. Even centuries after his death, David's reputation as a gifted musician and formidable warrior endures. A question naturally arises: "why did God choose

David over his more physically imposing elder brothers?"

In 1 Samuel 16, when prophet Samuel came to sanctify Jesse and his seven sons, David was conspicuously absent. Yet, by the narrative's end, the mantle of leadership unexpectedly fell upon him. This episode underscores a central truth: humans judge by outward appearances, but God discerns the heart. David's stature, height, or physical prowess were irrelevant. God chose him because He recognized David's unwavering obedience to His will.

It's no surprise then that God referred to David as "a man after His own heart" (Acts 13:22). In my interpretation, a heart like God's is one filled with devotion, gratitude, trust, and love. It is a heart that remains faithful regardless of circumstance. While David wasn't without flaws, God, in His sovereign wisdom, chose him nonetheless.

Like Goliath's shadow loomed over Israel, obscurity once veiled my own path. But just as a smooth stone sent ripples of victory through the valley, God's favor shattered my limitations. He plucked me from the unnoticed corners, and with a gentle hand, steered me towards a destiny far greater than I could have imagined.

And just as David rose to become Israel's golden king, leading them to their zenith, so too has God guided me to unexpected heights. His grace paved the way for achievements, not built on worldly accolades, but on the firm foundation of a heart surrendered to His will.

Why David? Why me? Maybe the answer lies not in outward appearances, but in God's unconventional choices. It's the heart that sings of devotion and beats with resolute faith, that truly captures God's attention. David wasn't perfect, and neither am I. But like him, I've learned that

God's favor flows from a wellspring of sovereignty, not our spotless records. He chooses not for our earthly glories, but for the melody of potential that resonates within us, waiting to be played.

This is my expedition, an attestation to the transformative power of grace, a hymn to the quiet, audacious whispers of God's plan. It's a story that echoes David's – a shepherd boy, crowned with purpose, not by earthly hands, but by the invisible love of the One who looks beyond the surface, and sees a heart yearning to serve.

The story of Esther, a young Jewish woman from the Persian Diaspora (Esther 2), also resonates deeply with me. Orphaned and raised by her uncle Mordecai, Esther's background offered little in the way of privilege or security. Imagine her feeling as a young girl, powerlessness, both for herself and for her fellow Jews living under foreign rule.

However, Esther refused to be defined by her circumstances or ethnicity. Instead of succumbing to despair or accepting the subjugation of her people, she displayed remarkable courage and strategic thinking. Throughout her trials, her faith in God's sovereignty remained steadfast.

It's important to recognize the divine hand at work in every step leading to Esther's triumph. From Queen Vashti's disobedience to King Ahasuerus, to Esther's selection as a candidate for queen, and even her favor with Hegai the custodian, each event appears orchestrated. Despite being an orphan raised by an enslaved uncle, Esther found herself unexpectedly on the path to royalty. Perhaps she, like David, the seemingly insignificant shepherd boy chosen by God, harbored a quiet faith. Unperturbed by the uncertainty of the future, she trusted in God's grace. When that grace fell upon her, her life shifted dramatically, not only for herself, but for her entire generation, as she became their unforeseen savior. These biblical narratives resonate deeply with my own story, for they offer a powerful testament to God's ability to work through even the most unexpected circumstances.

Like Esther, I tasted the bittersweet tang of a life on the margins, where shadows of doubt could easily eclipse hope. And like her, I also refused to let my limitations or background define me. In the quiet chambers of my heart, I too echoed her faith, whispering prayers to the same God who orchestrated her triumph. For I knew deep down that grace has a way of finding us and shifting us from obscurity to purpose; not just for ourselves, but for the ripple effect it creates in the lives of others.

For an orphan and outsider to suddenly stand on the precipice of becoming a queen, it's an evidence to the power of grace rewriting destinies. Just as David's sling toppled giants, Esther's quiet courage became the shield against her people's annihilation.

My story, like Esther's, is not just a proof to individual resilience, but to the divine hand that speaks courage into the hearts of the overlooked and underestimated. It's a story of faith taking flight that defied limitations and found purpose in a bigger design.

The Beginning of My Journey

I once wandered aimlessly, devoid of hope for the future. However, unknown to me, God had a plan. Regardless of one's background, whether privileged or disadvantaged (born with a silver spoon or a wooden one), a fundamental truth persists: our existence holds inherent meaning, and my life exemplifies this belief.

The world we inhabit is a complex place, brimming with mysteries and unforeseen occurrences. Yet, the divine creator possesses omniscience, perceiving all things from beginning to end. It becomes clear then, that life's accomplishments are not measured by socioeconomic status, family structure, or inherent abilities. Instead, the true measure lies in the grace bestowed upon each individual.

Lost in the fog of uncertainty and my hope as thin as dandelion fluff, I wandered as my future looked like a blank canvas mocking my aimless steps. Little did I know that even while I stumbled blindly in the shadows, that God was already crafting a masterpiece of my life.

He utilized trivial events in my childhood to fulfill His purpose in my life. One such instance involved a disagreement with my younger brother, who was prone to outbursts as a child. The disagreement concerned a traditional food called "akara." (Fried bean cakes). I vividly recall my mother returning from the market where she sold yams with six pieces of bean cakes and my younger brother desired all of them, which would have left me with none. When I objected to his selfish request, he attempted to take them by force, escalating the situation into a physical altercation. Traditionally, we would divide the six "akara" with the elder receiving four and the younger receiving two. However, my brother disregarded this custom. That childhood squabble over the akara nearly escalated into a potential serious injury. My mother and eldest brother were upset over our thuggish behavior. This event occurred when I was around twelve or thirteen years old and it coincided with the period when I had many suitors coming to my father to ask for my hand in marriage. Witnessing his sister's escalating troubles - a fight with her brother and a looming forced marriage - my eldest brother steps in. Determined to protect me, he embarks on a mission to alter my fate.

My potential suitors formed a diverse group, ranging from young men to older ones, farmers, individuals with disabilities, married men (seeking second wives), unmarried men, divorced men, unemployed men and even widowers. Ironically, this variety of suitors established me as the most fortunate young girl in our village. News of my prospects spread like wildfire, and I became the object of envy among my friends, many of whom lacked suitors altogether.

In those days, marriage was a family affair, and potential spouses were carefully chosen through consultation with an oracle. This process aimed to identify any potential problems in the future spouse's family, such as evil traits, mental illness, strange diseases, misconduct, or a history of untimely death. Needless to say, being associated with any of these issues could significantly hinder a family's marriage prospects.

Unlike the protections enshrined in Article 16 of the Universal Declaration of Human Rights, which guarantees the right to marry based on free consent, girls in my village had no such agency. Their fathers held absolute authority over their marital affairs. If a father desired to acquire cows, goats, or even fowls, he could essentially barter his daughter's hand in marriage to the man of his choosing. Female children were not fully integrated into the family structure. They held no rights of inheritance within their paternal homes, and the prevailing belief held that they truly belonged to their future husband's family.

Unfortunately, the concept of child abuse wasn't recognized within our traditional way of life. Fathers in particular, held absolute authority over their children's lives, with the right to make any decisions concerning their well-being.

For girls, education was a forbidden pursuit. It was seen as a waste of time and resources, as females were destined to be ultimately used in service to their husband's household. Females in our community were marginalized, and devalued. Their contributions and potential were largely unrecognized. **They were regarded as shadows flitting through the edges of society, destined to serve the men. Customarily, I was supposed to tread on the heels of my tradition, but my case was twirled by divine intervention.**

Though my family lacked wealth, they were deeply respected for their strong moral compass. My father meticulously evaluated each suitor. Ultimately choosing one of them in his thirties, primarily based on his youth and strength. My father believed this man's vigor would make him a valuable asset in his farm work.

The day the approved suitor arrived with his family,

bearing gifts of palm wine, kola nuts, and two bundles of tobacco for introductions, my eldest brother, Chief Solomon, also returned home. He had been living and working as a domestic helper in Abeokuta, the capital of Ogun State in western Nigeria, for many years. As the family heir, his presence was crucial at all family events, especially marriage ceremonies. Fortunately, he had recently been released from his service and was now living independently. Upon witnessing the commotion between my younger brother and I, and the unfolding marriage drama, my brother felt compelled to intervene on my behalf.

Prior to this pivotal day, I had expressed my desire for education in numerous letters to my brother. Despite possessing exceptional intelligence as a young girl, my father denied me the opportunity of a Western education. He also planned to marry me off at a young age, similar to my older sisters. My brother, however, vehemently opposed this arrangement. He engaged in a lengthy dialogue with my father, explaining the importance and benefits of education. He advocated for my right to attend school and asked that my father allow him to take me with him to Abeokuta. My father adamantly refused, clinging to traditional beliefs. He declared that none of his daughters would be "spoiled" by education, and cited financial constraints as an additional barrier. Following persistent discussions, my brother finally persuaded my father to relent. He agreed to release me on two conditions: firstly, that my brother maintain close supervision over me, and secondly, that I adhere to the family's strict moral code, which forbade premarital pregnancy.

Though my mother held a deep affection for us and yearned for our access to Western education, her influence as a woman was limited. She expressed her love and hopes through constant prayers for our well-being and by serving my father diligently with respect. The fight between my brother and I, once a childish memory, now resonated with deeper meaning. It was a reminder that even the smallest pebble can set in motion a grander design. The early marriage that loomed like a storm also became a strange twist of fate, a divine nudge in the right direction. Both occurrences were divinely orchestrated, as they became a turning point that paved the way for my liberation.

My Faith in a Higher Power

Lest I forget, my childhood unfolded under the shadow of two opposing forces: the darkness of ancestral gods worshiped by my father, and the warm light of God embraced by my mother. My father adhered to traditional practices, worshiping the deities revered by our ancestors for generations. However, this faith seemed to bring misfortune rather than blessings. I witnessed him repeatedly offer sacrifices of fowls and goats to appease these gods, yet our family endured a cycle of hardship. Instead of the promised protection, peace, good health, and prosperity, we faced a series of afflictions and untimely deaths that tragically claimed many family members, including my father at a young age.

Fortunately, my mother found solace in a different faith. She embraced Christianity and faithfully followed the teachings of Jesus Christ throughout her life. Her resolute devotion came at a cost. Due to her religious belief, she endured humiliation, brutal beatings, and even suffered broken bones. Yet, she remained steadfast in her faith, refusing to yield to these trials. We witnessed her tend to her wounds, but once recovered, she would pick up her Bible and return to church, undeterred by the potential consequences.

Witnessing my mother's firm devotion to God significantly impacted us. Inspired by her faith, my siblings and I decided to follow in her footsteps. She instilled in us the belief that ancestral worship represented darkness of the unknown, while Christianity offered the light of God's grace. She passionately explained the benefits of embracing this faith and living a life emulating the teachings of Jesus Christ. Her own life served as a powerful example. She extended love and care beyond the confines of our home, consistently demonstrating Christ-like behavior throughout her lifetime.

My mother served as a powerful role model, instilling in me the core principle that serving God is a constant duty, unfaltering in the face of adversity. Embracing my faith in Jesus Christ at a young age, I held fast to my belief with fixed conviction. Fueled by this newfound devotion, I actively participated in spreading the gospel of repentance alongside my fellow Christian friends throughout the village. This dedication to my faith continued even after relocating to the township with my brother. My belief and acceptance of Jesus Christ as my Lord and Savior laid the unshakeable foundation for the person I am today.

Recounting the events that led to my life's transformation

is undeniably an emotional experience. As children of God, we are created with a purpose, destined to fulfill a unique mission in life. However, this path is rarely without obstacles. Hindrances, challenges, and trials are inevitable, but in His hand, we are not pawns, but heroes in the making. This isn't just my story, it's a song for every child of God facing impossible odds. Submit your dreams to Him, dance to His rhythm, and watch as He paints your future with the vibrant hues of possibility. Once we place our faith in Him, anxieties dissipate, for it is His reputation, not ours, that is at stake.

As seen in my story, years later, the whirlwind has settled, the suitors a distant echo. But their parade remains a vibrant lesson – every encounter, every choice, and every brushstroke on the canvas of my life was guided by an unseen hand. My journey is a testament to the twists and turns of fate, that even beneath the most ordinary moments, life's grand design might be taking shape.

CHAPTER 3: LIFE IN ABEOKUTA 1989 -1999

Following the marriage histrionics in our village, I gripped my brother's hand as we boarded the rickety bus and embarked on a journey to Abeokuta, Ogun State, where he lived. The village, with its buzz of forced marriage and stifling traditions, felt like a jungle I had just escaped.

My brother was a kind but unpolished bachelor, who lived in a one-room "face-me-I-face-you" apartment (a form of communal housing), with a small attached storage unit that he converted into a room for me. My new accommodation lacked luxury, no plush carpets or silken pillows, just a lumpy raggedy twin sized mattress, laid bare on the floor. But compared to the dirt-caked mat and mosquito buffet I endured back in the village, this felt like a palace.

Moving from the village to the town was the first step on a path of significant change in my life. In my brother's household, I was no longer excluded from decision-making. Despite his modest income as a teacher, my brother generously provided me with 20 Nigerian Naira each week for groceries.

For the most part, we relied heavily on the reserves of *garri* (cassava flour) that I brought with me from the village. However, the soup condiments were different from the ones in the village. Despite my young age, I was entrusted with the task of managing our resources. With the 20 Naira each week, I strived to prepare a pot of egusi (melon seed) and okra soup. A key ingredient I ensured to include was "SOBONDE", the most affordable and, unfortunately, boniest fish available at the market. Escaping a choking hazard from these bones was a constant challenge. Our dependence on *garri* wasn't a preference, but rather a necessity due to its affordability. While variety in our meals was limited, we found contentment in what we had. In comparison to the village, where rice was a Christmas delicacy, I now had the privilege of enjoying it every other Sunday. Though I felt a sense of relief from the hardships of rural life, adapting to the urban environment proved challenging as well.

While in Abeokuta, my brother enrolled me in a public elementary school. At that time, I was about fourteen or fifteen years old. Despite the delay in my education, I cherished having the opportunity at all. Life in Abeokuta held great promise. I thrived in the academic environment, even being chosen as class monitor for my classes. This success culminated in an extraordinary opportunity during my fourth-grade year. I was selected to participate in a debate on Nigerian Television Authority (NTA), where I argued the proposition "What a man can do, a woman can do better" against a sixth-grader. Remarkably, I emerged victorious in this debate. The victory propelled me into the school's spotlight, but deep down, I remained a village girl, still searching for my own path.

My teenage years were a whirlwind of emotions as I grappled with self-discovery and societal integration. Eager to explore my surroundings, I ventured out frequently with my new found friends. One day, a female friend convinced me to attend what I believed was an African Cup of Nations soccer match held in Abeokuta that year. As the stadium gates partially opened, I found myself amidst a throng of thousands, possibly even millions, surging towards the narrow entrance. Before I could mutter a word, a stampede erupted. Trapped in the human press, I was lifted off my feet, unable to breathe or move. Managing to turn my head, I spotted my girlfriend caught in the same predicament. Gasping for air, I blurted out, "I'm dying!" Her immediate response was, "Me too!" Then, as abruptly as it began, the crowd parted, and I landed back on my feet.

In the aftermath, I saw several people lying motionless on the ground, including my girlfriend. Some were tragically deceased, while others received medical attention. Numb with shock, I watched as ambulances streamed in and out of the stadium in a blur. Once my friend regained consciousness, we fled the scene. That harrowing experience irrevocably severed my passion for soccer.

You might wonder why this experience holds significance in my narrative. It serves as a constant reminder of my brush with death, a promise I made to myself never to forget. The regretful truth is, I never informed my brother of my whereabouts that day, nor did I share the harrowing encounter with him. Upon returning home that evening, I spent a considerable amount of time contemplating the horrific ordeal. Filled with profound gratitude, I expressed my deepest appreciation to Almighty God for granting me another chance to live. **The near tragedy became a turning point, a stark reminder of life's fleeting beauty, urging me to savor every laugh, every breath, every step on this newfound path towards discovering who I truly was.**

My senior year in high school was marked by a profound loss. In 1997, my beloved father passed away in our village after a long battle with chronic asthma. His death plunged me into a deep well of grief. While I wasn't financially dependent on him, his passing left a void that I couldn't explain. My academic performance, previously characterized by straight A's, began to suffer. My grades slipped to a mix of B's, C's, and possibly one or two A's. Wracked with silent grief, I struggled with anxiety and panic attacks.

Thanks to my brother's tireless support, he enrolled me in private tutoring sessions. This allowed me to retake the West African Examination Council (WAEC) exams, the equivalent of a high school diploma, and achieve improved grades. Fueled by a desire for further education, I set my sights on a career in catering and hotel management. This field appealed to me, not only for its professional opportunities, but also for the possibility to enjoy good food. However, fate, through my brother's intervention, had a different path in store for me.

When I shared my career aspirations in catering and hotel management with my brother, he expressed reservations. He believed it wasn't the most suitable path for me. Instead, he proposed nursing, suggesting that if I excelled in the entrance exam, he would leverage his connections to facilitate my admission to the prestigious University College Hospital (UCH), Ibadan. Determined to succeed, I poured my efforts into studying. Thankfully, with my brother's guidance in navigating the then-complex admissions process, I was fortunate to be among the few accepted into the University in 1999. Although my career path shifted, guided by grief, family, and perhaps a higher purpose, in its place, blossomed the promise of caring for others, a path paved with compassion and healing.

My mother offered me a guiding principle during my teenage years: life is a trip she said, but as a young woman, its meaning remained elusive. However, with the passage of time and the maturation that comes with adulthood, I've come to find it a profound and endlessly fascinating concept. The notion of a journey is inherently subjective. For some, it signifies a literal voyage from one point to another, with a return to the origin. For others, it represents a more figurative race or process, akin to travel, filled with the inevitable trials, tribulations, and challenges that lie along the way. No matter what curveballs life throws your way, hold fast to your courage, focus, faith, and self-confidence. Remember, you possess the potential for greatness. Instead of succumbing to the urge to quit, seek the strength to persevere and the courage to endure. Through resilience, you'll discover the path God has laid out for you.

Don't give up! When things get tough, seek strength to keep going, and trust in God's plan. A wise religious leader observed that life is like a university set by God. Regardless of one's intellectual gifts, there are no shortcuts or double promotions, every course must be completed as each serves a purpose. This serves as a reminder: perseverance is the key. Those who abandon their goals in the face of difficulty are unlikely to achieve success. Conversely, those with a strong will to win never give up.

Looking back, my life wasn't always smooth sailing, my life was a rollercoaster – highs that made me whoop with joy, lows that felt like falling forever. But even if I could rewind the whole shebang, I wouldn't change a thing. Every twist, every stumble, brought me here, to this very second. And for that, I can only do one thing: bow my head and whisper a big, fat thank you to the Big God. He's been my guide, my rock, and I trust Him with the chapters yet to be written. The future is a mystery, but with faith and grit, I'm ready for whatever twists and turns He throws my way.

CHAPTER 4: BECOMING MRS. NWAEFUNA

My metamorphosis to *Mrs. Nwaefuna* began in 1999 at the University College Hospital, Ibadan, where I started my nursing career. In the year 2000, I encountered my husband in an extraordinary circumstance, one that defied easy explanation yet surely fit within God's divine plan. Our meeting took place at a medical unit where I spent many evenings after class offering words of encouragement to patients struggling with hopelessness. He wasn't a patient himself, but rather a visitor offering support to a fellow villager whose daughter had been tragically injured on her way back to her university campus.

Our friendship blossomed quickly; our connection was unexpected, like a twist in a well-worn story. He would often seek updates on the patient's progress, masking his true motivation for seeing me. Soon, our conversations stretched beyond medicine, morphing into something warm and familiar. We discovered joy in each other's company. He would eagerly wait for my visits to the hospital, and while my primary concern remained the patients, I admit to finding excuses to see him as well.

As our bond deepened, he revealed what felt unimaginable then: God had shown him I was his future partner, but there was a struggle. He had prayed for a smart, God-fearing woman with good character and a respectable career. However, while I fit the bill internally, my "big nose, fat legs, and short stature" clashed with his initial image. He wrestled with these notions, comparing me to other women who'd pursued him, even one who offered an engagement ring. Ultimately, faith prevailed. Apparently, God whispered to him in a vision, "look beyond the surface; her true beauty lies within." After that encounter, he recognized me as his divinely chosen partner, the "raw gold" he was meant to refine, just like gold miners transform their precious finds.

Years later, the evidence speaks for itself. We are still standing together, a testament to a love that transcended initial perception and embraced a deeper connection guided by something beyond ourselves.

Before meeting my husband, college life for me was starkly different from my classmates. While they seemed to have it all, juggling boyfriends and comfortable lifestyles, I struggled with abject poverty. Food, clothing, even basic necessities were luxuries I couldn't afford. The little I had came from my brother, who himself had started a family and had his plate full.

Loneliness, dejection, isolation, hardship and anger gnawed at me. Often ridiculed by classmates; one night, a nagging hunger drove me to a desperate plea. At about 11 pm, I begged my roommate for leftover food, swallowing my pride just to eat. Each day was a fight for survival, but my faith in God remained steadfast. My only solace was found in church and spreading the word of God. I made a vow: to never compromise my values for money or material things. Even if life remained tough, I wouldn't stray from my faith. It was a desperate prayer, hoping God would see me through.

Then, at the perfect moment, destiny intervened. My husband entered my life, showering me with love I had never known. He tirelessly ensured my comfort, and soon, envy replaced the scorn of my classmates. The whispers started, wondering what a man like him could see in "a lowlife girl" like me. Some even tried to win him over, oblivious to the unbreakable bond we shared. My husband was more than my love; he was my protector and still is; a proof that faith could rewrite even the harshest stories.

A bittersweet note to our story is the passing of the patient who brought us together. It's tempting to question God's plan in moments of sadness, but even through tragedy, He weaves his wonders. Sometimes, even painful events play a part in His perfect design for our lives. It's not always easy to understand, but remember: God works in mysterious ways.

As the Bible verse (1 Corinthians 1:28 *The Passion Translation*, TPT) says, He often chooses the overlooked, the "nobodies", to achieve extraordinary things. He uses the seemingly insignificant to outshine the powerful - that is my story. He brought us together through an unfortunate event, ultimately leading to an incredible love story.

Our journey wasn't without hurdles. When my husband announced his intention to marry me, my brother needed to investigate his family background, to rule out certain beliefs before approving our marriage. The thought of losing him, my only real friend, filled me with dread. Thankfully, the investigation yielded positive results.

Next came the traditional marriage process. Starting with an introduction ceremony in Abeokuta, where I lived with my brother. Afterwards, we met with my kinsmen in the village. Various meetings between his family and mine followed, fulfilling all customary requirements. Finally, on February 21, 2003, we celebrated our wedding at my father's compound, officiated by our local church pastor.

Before our wedding, dark signs emerged. My younger brother dreamt of a menacing cow-like figure named "dark-able", prompting our family to fast and pray. The night before the ceremony, during a vigil at my father's compound, a huge scorpion inexplicably wanted to attack me, but my sister-in-law bravely killed it.

On our journey to my husband's hometown after the wedding, another unsettling event occurred. An image resembling a dark cow appeared in the middle of the road, visible only to my husband and I . Though it seemed to brush the car, our driver and my two siblings sitting by me remained unaware. My husband yelled for the driver to stop, while I called out to Jesus severally, feeling like I was in a surreal movie. Thankfully, the car stopped just in time, and the image vanished across the road. Remembering my brother's dream and our prayers, we interpreted this as a spiritual obstacle defeated by our faith and prayers.

Arriving in my husband's town, the lack of celebration was evident. There was no electricity, despite my husband paying for a generator that wouldn't work even with the tank filled with fuel; the DJ couldn't play music, plunging the event into darkness and silence. People struggled to see each other. After a brief encounter with the guests, my husband and I went to bed; after all, our marriage itself is the most important thing and not the ceremonial part.

The following day, my siblings returned to our village,

while my husband and I went back to Ibadan, our home at that time. The dream of the dark cow, the scorpion, and the disturbing encounter on the road lingered in my thoughts, leaving me apprehensive about the future. I grappled with the question of what would have transpired if God had not revealed the dream and its images to my husband and I. The inexplicable act of malice against me, an innocent person, fueled further confusion. Could ancestral forces, as some might believe, have been involved? The more I contemplated these uncertainties, the less I comprehend the unseen forces at play. But amidst the confusion, one anchor held firm - my faith. I clung to the unwavering belief that God's sovereignty stretched over every twist and turn of life's battles. Once revealed in dreams and visions, God's power would continue to thwart the unseen dangers, and the hidden threats. In the face of the unknown, I chose to trust, to hold onto the quiet melody of hope that hummed beneath the surface of doubt.

Our journey to marital bliss wasn't a smooth path bathed in perpetual sunshine. It was punctuated by moments of darkness that we overcame together. These challenges stand as silent testaments to the enduring strength of our love, the steady support of our family, and our shared faith. They are forever engraved into the tapestry of our narrative.

The path ahead might have been obscured, but I knew one thing - I wouldn't walk it alone. With faith as my shield and God as my guiding light, I was ready to face whatever awaited, hand in hand with the man who called me his wife.

CHAPTER 5: DREAM TAKES FLIGHT

About a year into our relationship, before we tied the knot, my husband, a man with big dreams and vision, shared his lifelong desire to live and raise a family in America. He needed my support, and I readily agreed, having heard wonderful things about the country. Excitement surged through me. America, the land of endless possibilities, the promise of a better tomorrow! It felt like fate itself was nudging us forward. Soon after, hand in hand, we entered a bank, his determination crackling in the air, as he surprised me with a lottery ticket, with our names already printed as "Mr. and Mrs." even though we weren't married yet. He later felt he should change it to only my name. Yet, something extraordinary happened, as if the universe itself conspired with our dreams, the bank relented, citing potential fraud concerns. But miraculously, they agreed after further discussion, as if guided by a higher power.

And then, something incredible happened! Out of millions of participants in the 2001 visa lottery, I was chosen. Not just for one country, but for America, Canada, and Australia! The decision was easy, though. My husband's dream, his unwavering focus on America, became our reality. News of our lottery win spread like wildfire, igniting envy and suspicion in some corners, and in the hearts of some. Whispers filled the air, and immediately turned to gossip, casting shadows across our path. Are unseen forces working against us or could it be ancestral forces back at play, slamming doors of opportunity?, I queried.

Finances dwindled, support evaporated, and doubt began to gnaw at the edges of our hope. People gossiped about my husband's dream, scoffing and doubting his ability to achieve it. "Dreamer," they sneered, their words a bitter cocktail of disbelief and scorn. "Let's see how he will make it to America," they scoffed, with their laughter echoing through our narrow streets. Despite all the happenings, my husband and I held onto our faith like a lifeline. Our story, woven into the fabric of our lives, mirrored that of a young boy named Joseph in the Bible, a young man who, despite his brothers' cruelty, held onto his God-given dreams of greatness. Joseph had a powerful dream. He saw sheaves of wheat bowing down to him, then dreamt of the sun, moon, and stars doing the same. His siblings, filled with envy, mocked him and eventually sold him into slavery.

Despite hardship and injustice, Joseph remained faithful. His strong character, his connection to God, and his fixed belief in his dreams guided him through every trial. Even though his brothers tried to prevent his destiny, Joseph's dreams eventually came true. He rose to become the Prime Minister of Egypt, saving countless lives through his wisdom and leadership. His story taught us that God's plans for us unfold in His perfect timing. Even when faced with challenges, our faith and determination can lead us to our true purpose. Just like Joseph, with God, all things are possible, no matter how impossible they may seem.

My husband wouldn't give up his pursuit of the American dream. He sold everything - the vibrant lifeblood of his cyber cafe, the promising shares, car, and even the cell phones that connected us to the world were sold for a meager amount, yet we continued to struggle to afford the visa fees, let alone the plane ticket. After much struggle we managed to buy my flight ticket with divine provision.

But a new challenge arose, we had no family or friends in the United States. Seven months pregnant with our first daughter, anxiety gnawed at my bones. The fear of losing that opportunity was shattering. We clung to our faith, but the stress made me very sick. My heart ached not just for our stalled dream, but for the tiny life stirring within me. The burden of finding a landing spot in a vast, unknown land, devoid of my family comfort or friends, felt like a weight threatening to crush me.

Undeterred, we researched shelters, but the process seemed overwhelming for a pregnant woman. In desperation, we even considered going to the police station upon arrival in the United States, hoping for a miracle. We navigated the murky waters of doubt, our faith, our compass, and our love, our anchor. We toiled, we prayed, we fought for every inch of progress, our firm determination became a beacon in the darkness. And finally, after months of struggle, God intervened, and doors began to open. My husband's brother who resides in Botswana suggested we contact his wife's sister-in-law who lives in New York City. This led us to Mrs Rosemary who miraculously solved our problem.

On September 7, 2003, my husband's birthday, I made my entrance into the United States. Fear gave way to relief, my weary heart found solace in Rosemary's warm embrace. It was a humble beginning, a single room in a bustling city, but it was home. A stepping stone on the path we had carved with hope and faith, a path that finally seemed bathed in the golden light of possibility.

The rest, as they say, is history. But our story is not just about defying odds or achieving the impossible. It's about the unwavering power of dreams, the unwavering strength of faith, and the unwavering love that binds two souls together in the face of adversity. It's a testament to the fact that even in the darkest of nights, the sun always rises, and even the most impossible dreams can take flight, carried on the wings of hope and the unwavering belief in the divine.

As I close this chapter, I can't help but share a glimpse into the shadows that lingered behind our dream while in Nigeria. Jealousy, like a poisonous vine, snaked its way through our lives. Some close friends of my husband who shared meals and laughter within our home, couldn't stomach his success. "We all went to school together", one of them voiced, bitterness dripping from his words. "Now you got married to a nurse, and not only that, but she also won the American lottery; let me be honest-not everyone is happy for your success".

Another person we had sheltered and fed, scurried out of our lives like a frightened rat the moment the whispers of the American visa lottery reached his ears. His betrayal stung, especially since he was one of the many we had helped along the way. Yet, instead of gratitude, he joined the chorus of doubt, sneering that my husband was a fool, throwing everything away for a woman who will leave him in a heartbeat for another man in America. "Loser", he spat, venom lacing his voice. "Over my dead body will Victor ever set his feet in America", he said. And, in a twist as unsettling as it was eerie, his wish seemed to grant itself. That individual died mysteriously shortly before my husband made his entrance into the United States. It makes one wonder, doesn't it? But who are we to judge what happened?

Despite those voices, we held onto our faith and belief in a brighter future. We understood that negativity often surrounds those who dare to dream big. The story of Joseph, from the Bible, exemplifies this truth. He faced envy and betrayal, yet ultimately achieved his God-ordained purpose.

Who says it's an abomination to dream beyond the confines of our situations or imagine greatness. In fact, when you don't dream or imagine yourself in the mirror of greatness, that is when limitations take root, and once you are captured in the mindset of mediocrity, it becomes impossible to believe the possible.

Throughout Joseph's trials, he never faltered. His steadfast faith and his unwavering spirit, shone through every hardship. He endured betrayal, slavery, and despair, and his resilience was a testament to his absolute belief in God's plan. And just as Joseph's dreams ultimately led him to become the prime minister of Egypt, our dream too, refused to be extinguished.

Joseph's story is a graphic depiction of the great truth in Romans 8:28 *King James Version* (KJV)- "And we know that all things work together for good to them that love God, to them who are called according to his purpose." Even in the face of envy, betrayal, loss, and mystery, faith held firm. We agreed to the belief that God's hand guided our path, and led us through the shadows.

The whispers of doubt, the sting of envy, were mere pebbles on the path to our destiny. For with God, all things are possible - a truth that resonated deep within our hearts. We knew with a certainty that our journey, like Joseph's, was divinely orchestrated. The obstacles and the trials were not roadblocks, but stepping stones that led us closer to the fulfillment of our dreams.

This chapter is not just about the statement of our American dream, but also a narrative of evidence to the steady power of faith in the face of doubt. It is a reminder that sometimes, the greatest victories are born not from sunshine and cheers, but from the quiet conviction that through hardship and heartache, God's purpose, not ours, leads us to the shores of our dreams.

CHAPTER 6: NAVIGATING AMERICA

Unlike some, I didn't have pockets overflowing with cash when I entered America. My move from Nigeria to America wasn't just about money, though that was a big part of it. Back home in Nigeria, life was tough, Jobs were scarce, crime was high, and opportunities seemed few and far between. As a newly minted nurse, I earned about $9 a month, barely enough to support my husband and I, let alone a baby on the way. Growing up in a poor community, the thought of staying in that cycle filled me with dread. That's why I fully supported my husband's dream of finding a better life abroad.

The reality of landing in America was a culture shock so intense, it knocked the wind out of me. It was like stepping into another world. The line at immigration was enormous, and everyone seemed to be talking at once. Everything was overwhelming, a labyrinth with no map, a symphony I couldn't decipher. Their accents sounded strange, different from the ones I knew from Hollywood movies. I couldn't help but feel a little lost. My naivety wasn't for lack of wit, but for a lack of a hand to hold. Alone, black, and African, I felt totally out of place. I was a lone leaf swept into a whirlwind of unfamiliarity.

Days melted into each other, a blur of searching and struggling to fit into this intricate puzzle of a country.

Everything felt so different and so confusing. But I knew staying alone wouldn't help. So, I started connecting with other Nigerians, specifically those in the church located close to where I lived. Mingling with faces who spoke the language of home, and those who understood my background, was comforting to my loneliness.

A few weeks after arriving, someone suggested I get prenatal care at the North Central Bronx hospital. I had no idea how to get there, what insurance was, or how I would get the funds to pay. But I figured things out, step by step, until I reached my destination.

The hospital, with a temple of fluorescent lights and hushed voices, welcomed me with an unexpected comfort. An angel in scrubs, sent by providence, guided me through the registration labyrinth that took hours, going from department to department. I didn't eat any breakfast or drink water, but I was just happy to be getting care and soon giving birth to an "American citizen" in an American hospital, "what a dream come through!".

The first six months were a test of faith and grit. Jobless, I leaned on my husband's resolute support, traveling from Nigeria to another African country to send me money, since doing it directly from Nigeria wasn't possible. His every dollar was a tiny spark in the darkness, as we continued to build our American dream, brick by brick, sweat by tear, hope by hope.

This is not just a tale of landing in America; it's a testament to the resilience of the human spirit, the unyielding power of dreams, and the quiet triumph of faith in the face of the unknown. In a land painted bright with possibilities, we found our place, not just on a map, but in the tapestry of a life we could only have dared to dream.

On December 2, 2003, a biting wind whipped through the city, carrying the remnants of a harsh storm. It was the day of my follow-up appointment with the midwife. I lacked a car, so I had to rely on public transportation. After several bus transfers, I finally arrived at the hospital, feeling the chill seep through my clothes.

My midwife's office was on a higher floor of the building. I took the elevator down after seeing her to grab a quick coffee and a bagel for breakfast in the lobby. Just as I took the first bite of the bagel, labor decided to make its surprise debut! An unmistakable gush of water down my legs sent me into a panicked sprint back to the elevator. Bursting into the midwife's office again, I breathlessly explained what had happened. With practiced efficiency, she ushered me into the delivery room. In that moment, the chaotic events felt strangely orchestrated, as if divinely guided by an unseen power.

With my husband still in Nigeria and Mrs. Rosemary away in school in another city, I felt utterly helpless. The only comfort I had was the belief that God was by my side. Stuck in the hospital room, the hours of labor stretched on, each contraction a lonely battle. A kind nurse asked if I had anyone to call, but in a voice rasped with exhaustion, I whispered, "I have no family, I'm here with God." The nurse's gaze held a flicker of disbelief, perhaps mistaking my faith for the delirium of labor. Her surprise gaze and her doubt of my sanity, stung, but I knew my truth.

The room blurred around me, my strength was draining away like water down a drain. Every ounce of energy left was focused on pushing, on breathing, and on fighting for life. My stomach convulsed with spasms, bile rising acidity in my throat. Kneeling by the toilet, I emptied my stomach. No one came, no comforting hand reached out.

I don't know how long I laid there, trapped in my own exhaustion, but I could only whisper "nurse, nurse", my voice barely audible. Time morphed into an endless loop of pain and fatigue. Then, as if lifted by a prayer, a figure materialized in the doorway. A nurse rushed in, finding me slumped on the floor, she gently led me to the shower, hoping that warm water would revive me. Under the warm spray, my muscles loosened, a quiver of strength returned.

The night stretched on, each contraction a tidal wave battering my bones, but I battled on, fueled by a primal instinct and a whispered prayer. And then, by dawn the next morning, my baby made her entry into the world. Relieved, I called Mrs. Rosemary, who showered me with congratulations and promised to arrange for our return home. On December 5, 2003, a snowstorm raged outside the hospital. Despite the blizzard, Mrs. Rosemary kept her word. Arriving with a friend, they drove us safely home, a warm haven amidst the wintry chaos.

Two months into motherhood, a terrifying dream woke me up from sleep in a cold sweat. In it, I saw our little girl (Laura), weak and thin with diarrhea. A strange, invisible force tried to snatch her away, but I clung to her tight, praying with all my heart. Then, as if by magic, the force disappeared and a brand-new, healthy baby floated down from the sky to replace her. I woke up with a pounding heart, wondering what it could mean.

To my surprise, Mrs. Rosemary, who was in another city at the time, had a similar dream! Even before I could call her to tell her about mine, she had called a pastor to pray for me. I was so shaken by the experience that I needed answers, desperately trying to understand what these dreams meant.

I kept asking the Holy Spirit for interpretation. The next day, I had a strange experience where I relived some of my pregnancy dreams, including one where an old woman touched my belly. I heard in my spirit that my baby was changed in the womb and the new baby was a replacement from God. Remarkably, my baby (Laura) was also named "Nkechinyerem", meaning God's gift to me even before the dream. This was another evidence that God indeed is with me and that He knows the end from the beginning.

That experience opened my eyes to the idea that Christians face spiritual battles every day, even if we cannot see the attacker. Our struggles, I understood, would come in different shapes and sizes, each battle unique in its degree of intensity. Spiritual warfare is not physical or mental, neither is it fighting with fists or arguing, but more like a hidden war against external forces we can't understand; and this kind of war requires a supernatural counterforce to emerge victorious. Within that quiet triumph, I found not just answers, but an unshakeable certainty: even in the darkest dream, there is always light, waiting to be found.

Beyond the Green Card

Adapting to the American system after having my first baby was like stepping onto a different planet with a mountain to climb. And not having the right information and right people around me for direction made it even harder. As a new mom, balancing my baby's needs with my own, while figuring out a whole new world, was pretty nerve-wracking. No family was around to help, so I relied on the kindness of some church members. Even with their support, buying baby food and clothes felt impossible.

Although I came into the United States with a green card, that wasn't a guarantee or a ticket to comfort living. But you know what? In the face of uncertainty, sometimes the universe throws you a lifeline. Luckily, I wasn't completely alone.

One day, I met a kind Nigerian woman who changed everything. She introduced me to something called "food stamps" and "WIC benefits". I jumped on the bus that same day with my baby to our local DSS office to apply for them. The process was relatively rigorous but I had no problem going through the stress. Luckily for me, I was successful at the end and after a month or so, I started receiving WIC checks for my baby's milk and financial assistance from the U.S. Government, for my baby and I.

An unforgettable experience occurred one freezing winter day, as I waited at the bus stop with my baby, bundled only in a thin shawl and my spring jacket. The bone-chilling cold escaped my notice, due to the weight of my worries. Fear and despondency had numbed me to the world around me. Lost in my thoughts, I didn't even realize the temperature had sunk below zero degrees Fahrenheit. All I knew was the urgent need to get my baby to the doctor. While I stood alone shivering, suddenly, a car pulled up and a kind African-American woman stepped out. Handing me a five-dollar bill, she said, "This weather isn't safe for you and your baby; I was once in your shoes and I remember what it's like." Before I could thank her, she was gone. With tears in my eyes, I hailed a taxi and rushed to the hospital, grateful for this unexpected act of kindness. God had sent a stranger to answer my unspoken prayer. A stranger became an angel, her generosity was a reminder that we are never truly alone in our struggles.

While I thought that things were easing up a little bit, an unexpected challenge arose. The whispers of uncertainty started filling the air at Mrs. Rosemary's house, circumstances beyond her control, which necessitated me leaving her house. Worry gnawed at me: "where would I go with a newborn?" But the answer arrived miraculously, almost immediately. The Arogundades, guided by divine faith, opened their hearts and home to me and my baby. They became our family, even offering the first $100 I needed to complete a Home Health Aide (HHA) training. Armed with my new certificate, I found a job, but my joy turned to worry one day, when my babysitter called with alarming news; my daughter had fallen and injured herself. Overhearing the frantic call exchange, the patient I was caring for, with surprising kindness, insisted I leave immediately despite not completing my shift. Grateful for his concern, I rushed to my babysitter's house.

Unaware of the company's policies, I clocked out on the street using the public phone. Later that day, the cruel reality of the situation hit. A phone call from the main office confirmed my fears: I had been fired. Devastated, I was left jobless and income-less, with only my baby's wide, innocent eyes looking up at me. The weight of our uncertain future felt unbearable.

Facing unemployment after being fired, I found solace in the words of a fellow church member who suggested a bold plan: to send my daughter to Nigeria to bond with her father while I focus on studying for the NCLEX exam, the key to becoming a licensed registered nurse in the United States. He even offered to store my belongings in his spare space.

At first, the idea seemed ludicrous. Leaving my two-year-old behind, especially in a country with its challenges, seemed unimaginable. Images of mosquito bites and malaria threats filled my mind. But then, I remembered the years my husband had spent away from his wife and first child, the longing he must have felt. With a deep breath, I decided to trust this unconventional path.

I wanted my husband to be part of our daughter's childhood fostering, I wanted him to partake in those special moments. So I traveled to Nigeria with our daughter. It turned out that our journey to Nigeria was a medium to rescue my husband from loneliness induced depression.

He bought the lottery ticket. While the lottery win enabled my immigration to America, a frustrating five-year wait followed before I was finally reunited with him. Does that sound right? Probably not. The complexities of the immigration process can be truly daunting for those who haven't experienced them firsthand.

Life sometimes throws curveballs, sometimes ones that seem impossible to handle. The weight of the situation can crush our spirit, rob us of resources, and leave us feeling utterly alone. Yet, amidst the chaos, there's a truth that shines bright: God never burdens us beyond our capacity to endure.

This isn't just a comforting notion; it's a core principle of God's character. He reigns supreme, holding absolute power and authority over all creation. No matter how confusing things get, His Word and promises remain steadfast.

Ephesians 1:11 beautifully reminds us, "He works all things out in conformity with the counsel of His will." This verse has been my anchor in countless storms, a light guiding me through the darkest hours.

My return from Nigeria was like stepping through a new door. At the Kaplan review center in bustling Manhattan, another Nigerian woman shared vital information that changed my situation for the better. She connected me with an agent who helped me secure a limited permit license, allowing me to work as a licensed practical nurse (LPN) while studying for my registered nurse certification exam. This opportunity meant better pay than my previous HHA position, enough to finally rent an attic space of my own.

Fueled by renewed determination, I embarked on a rigorous course of study. By the grace of God, I aced the exam and secured a fulfilling position with the State of New York. My sights were now set on building a better life for my family. With the purchase of my first car and a more comfortable apartment, I awaited my husband and daughter's long-awaited arrival with a mix of anticipation and hope.

As a Christian, I believe God works through life's challenges, to demonstrate His supremacy in our lives. Yet, within our bustling world, filled with noise and distractions, discerning His voice can feel like finding a single whisper amidst a roaring crowd.

God doesn't limit Himself to a single method. He may speak in the quiet moments of reflection, through the twists and turns of our circumstances, or even through the voices of others. Some individuals, like fleeting echoes, may divert our attention. Others, however, serve as divine megaphones, amplifying His will. It becomes our crucial task to discern these genuine messengers from the distractors.

It's also important to recognize that God works according to His divine plan. He interlace His purpose into the tapestry of our lives through various means. This can be through the events we experience or the people we meet along the way.

As the Bible reminds us in Proverbs 16:9, *Amplified Version* (AMP), "A man's heart plans his way, but the Lord establishes his steps." While we may have aspirations and desires, ultimately, God guides our journey.

Sharing my story feels necessary because the road to success often differs from our initial expectations. It can be a long, solitary journey, lined with obstacles and setbacks. These paths can test our faith and patience, forcing us to navigate unexpected turns.

However, my personal experience has revealed that these obstacles and failures are not meant to break us. Instead, they serve as teachers, encouraging adaptability, flexibility, and the ability to leverage change to our advantage. They keep us nimble, fostering a growth mindset that motivates us to learn and evolve.

Remember, your life experiences help shape who you are. It's the uniqueness of your personal attributes that reveals the essence of your being. So, when the road seems long and the obstacles loom large, remember this: "your journey is yours alone, its contours are shaped by the stories inscribed within you." Embrace the detours, for they hold the potential for transformation. Let the failures be your teachers and catalysts for growth. And above all, never lose sight of the beauty that emerges from your unique experiences for they hold the power to refine and strengthen you, leading you closer to your true potential.

CHAPTER 7: A JOYFUL REUNION/ A NEW CHAPTER BEGINS

For five long years, I navigated the bustling streets of New York City alone, despite being married. But in September 2009, our family circle finally became complete. My husband and daughter arrived in America, and a wave of relief washed over me. My heart finally found its missing beat.

The hardship of being separated from a loved one for a long time is undeniable. Anyone who's ever been apart from their love for that long knows it's no cakewalk. Sleepless nights were a constant shadow of sadness, and enough anxiety to fill a Broadway theater – yep, I had them all. Scientific studies even confirm this, revealing that long-term distance can lead to sleep problems, depression, and anxiety. But despite the hardships, I'm grateful for the chance to share my story.

Ideally, couples shouldn't be apart for more than six months to a year, at most. Even with the distance, communication is crucial to navigating feelings of loneliness, missing intimacy, and emotional and physical stress. In my case, however, these resources were unavailable. I lacked even a stable place to live, let alone the privacy needed for communication.

The vast distance of over 6,000 miles separated me from my husband. Back then, I couldn't even afford a calling card. In that time of need, a wonderful Christian brother and friend, Pastor Yemi, stepped in with incredible kindness. He took it upon himself to buy me calling cards, allowing me to speak with my husband nearly every other day. This act of generosity may seem ordinary to some, but for me, Pastor Yemi was a godsend. He fulfilled a crucial need in that difficult time, a lifeline that kept me connected to my consort.

The emotional toll of separation from a loved one, particularly a spouse, is a complex and multifaceted experience. As a mental health professional, I'm keenly aware that while separation anxiety is often associated with childhood, it can profoundly impact adults as well. This is especially true for couples with strong emotional bonds.

My husband and I have always shared an incredibly close bond. Perhaps too close, as we had become accustomed to being by each other's side constantly. Even simple errands felt incomplete without the other. So, when the search for better opportunities necessitated separation after our marriage, it wasn't just difficult – it was devastating and overwhelming.

Facing long separations requires immense courage, unwavering determination, patience, and a deep connection to one's faith. During this challenging time, I encountered numerous temptations and moments of humiliation. However, I held fast to my faith, refusing to let my emotions cloud my judgment. I understood that succumbing to these feelings would only make things more difficult in the long run.

This is just the beginning of our family's story in the land of opportunity. Join me as we navigate the streets of New York, bridge the gap of years apart, and build a life together, one hug at a time.

Before my husband immigrated to America, I visited Nigeria several times without conceiving. More than six years had passed since the birth of our first child, and we longed to grow our family. However, upon his arrival, it felt like a blessing straight from Genesis 1:28: "God blessed them and said to them, 'Be fruitful and multiply and fill the earth'." Our family quickly grew from three to four, and then to a joyful seven.

God's promise to expand our family unfolded in a way that surpassed our wildest dreams. He bestowed upon us more blessings than we could have ever dared to ask for. Each of our children's births was marked by a remarkable event, a testament to God's grace in our lives.

The arrival of our second daughter came seven years after our first. I vividly recall laying in the hospital bed during her labor, weak and pale. Fear gripped my husband, yet his faith held strong as he continued praying. At one point, he feared for my life. The delivery stalled – I lacked the strength to push further, and the baby's heart rate plummeted. Thankfully, the attending Chinese doctor made a swift and decisive clinical choice, employing a vacuum extraction to safely deliver our daughter.

After our daughter's dramatic delivery, the medical team expressed concern about her left hand. They worried she might have limited mobility. Undeterred, my husband countered their statement with unwavering faith. "Don't worry," he declared, "she will move it." Remarkably, life seemed to surge through her arm almost instantaneously.

She not only began moving it that day, but continues to use it fully to this day. We view this as a proof of God's miraculous intervention.

Vacuum-assisted delivery, while helpful, can carry some risks. These include potential infections and injuries to the mother's birth canal, as well as skull fractures, bleeding in the eyes or brain, and jaundice for the baby. Thankfully, neither of us experienced any of these complications. This is a sign of God's grace, a divine hand guiding the skilled medical team to achieve a successful outcome and avert potential catastrophe.

A Time of Dual Concern

Two years after our second daughter's birth, I conceived our first son. During his pregnancy, my mother came to visit from Nigeria. Unfortunately, unknown to me, she was suffering from high blood pressure. Blinded by the stress of my own pregnancy, I didn't realize the seriousness of her condition until she tragically suffered a major stroke.

Hospitalized and facing the demands of my own late-term pregnancy, I spent countless days and nights by her side. It was a period of immense emotional strain, a time when I juggled the anxieties of childbirth with the worry for my mother's health.

Devastating news struck as doctors revealed my mother had suffered a brain hemorrhage, and due to her age, surgery wasn't an option. The only hope was for the bleeding to stop naturally, leaving her in the hospital for an uncertain duration.

Internally and externally, stress consumed me. The

fear of losing my mother intertwined with anxieties about what my family back home would think. Would they suspect foul play? Mentally and physically drained, I reached out to everyone in my network, informing them of the situation and pleading for their prayers.

With unwavering support, my family, friends, and well-wishers immediately launched into a fervent prayer vigil. Thankfully, as if an answer to their collective faith, the bleeding stopped miraculously the next day. The medical team, astonished by her rapid recovery, couldn't explain it. For us, it was a clear confirmation of the Lord's intervention. In that hushed room, amidst the hum of machines and the quiet rustle of hope, I witnessed the Lord's hand once again, gently steering us back from the precipice. That was not just a medical marvel; it was a testament to the unyielding power of faith in the midst of chaos. It's the story of a daughter, a mother, a son still cradled in my womb, and the divine hand that wove them all into a shade of resilience and grace.

Shortly after my mother's release from the hospital, I went into labor. However, the stress of the previous ordeal had taken its toll. Exhausted and overwhelmed, I struggled to push, but the baby's weight added to the difficulty. The attending doctor, instead of offering the support I desperately craved, sat and watched me struggle. Then, in a moment of callous disregard, he uttered a chilling statement: "If you don't push, your f—king child will die."

Alone and vulnerable, I felt a desperate need for a higher power. I had asked my husband earlier to go home and be with the other children and my mother. In that desolate room, with the doctor's words hanging in the air, I remembered the ultimate physician, my ever present helper in time of crisis. A surge of unexpected strength coursed through me, and I cried out "Jesus!" with a force that shook the room. In that instant, my son arrived without any further delay, healthy and whole. Only then did the doctor and a nurse approach my bedside to attend to me and my baby.

Finding Forgiveness

The physician's insensitive remarks haunted me for a long time; the sting of his cruelty was a constant ache. The thought of legal action crossed my mind, but then, a sense of peace washed over me. The Holy Spirit reminded me of the divine deliverance, I had just experienced a miraculous delivery. He reminded me of how God had intervened in my moment of despair. Vengeance, I realized, was not mine to seek. Instead, I chose to heal, to find solace in the knowledge that I was not alone. At that moment, healing began, allowing me to move forward.

Forgiveness is a powerful act of letting go of anger and resentment for someone who has wronged you. It's not necessarily forgetting what happened, but rather releasing the negativity associated with it. To successfully find forgiveness, we must understand its benefits: forgiveness allows you to move on and find peace. Holding onto anger can be emotionally draining. It's okay to process your feelings and acknowledge your hurt and anger, but don't bottle them up. While you hurt, consider the other person's perspective, maybe he acted out of fear or ignorance. Work on letting go of the need for revenge because focusing on revenge will keep you tied to the past. Instead, forgive your offender and move forward.

Unexpected Blessings

My husband and I initially decided to forgo having more children, but our plans shifted. We were informed it wasn't yet the right time to close that chapter. Two years later, I received a powerful dream. God revealed a vision of a baby boy, and I distinctly heard Him say He was granting us another son.

Sharing this dream with my husband, a remarkable coincidence came to light. He confided in me about a vision he'd had even before our first son's conception. In his dream, two boys approached him and asked, "Do you love Jesus?" His response was a question of faith: "If I don't love Jesus, who will I love?"

Just a month after my dream, as I was preparing for my appointment, for an IUD insertion, my menstrual cycle stopped. That unexpected development became a clear sign – our family was about to grow once more.

While initially surprised by the news, my husband's reaction shifted. His initial echo of joy was silenced by the memory of his own forgotten vision, he reacted with a storm of anger and frustration as he yelled, "Go find your menses wherever you've misplaced it," refusing to accept the impossible. Soon after, he recognized his emotional turmoil, and eventually sought forgiveness as he knelt in prayers.

This experience deepened his faith. He embraced the prospect of another son, proposing the name "Chukwuka," which means "God is greater" – a fitting middle name reflecting his newfound acceptance and faith in God's plan.

Unlike our other kids who are Bronx natives, Nathan Chukwuka entered the world here, in Upstate New York. His arrival was a bit early, at 37 weeks gestation. Though technically considered "late-premature", he defied the label by being perfectly formed and healthy. This is nothing but an absolute power of God at play. Most late-premature babies need some extra monitoring, and some often face fewer challenges but our son's case is different. His dedication ceremony took place at the Redeemed Christian Church of God Restoration Assembly, House of Favor, Albany New York. The meaning of his name, "Chukwuka" (God is greater), has proven remarkably prophetic, guiding both his words and actions within our family.

Even at a young age, Nathan has exhibited a deep sensitivity, both physically and spiritually. As you'll discover in Chapter Ten, a remarkable event unfolded when he secretly made a challenging request from God, and his wish was granted.

CHAPTER 8: MY EDUCATION AND CAREER JOURNEY

Growing up, societal norms dictated a narrow path for females in my community. Girls were excluded from influential discussions and relegated to endless chores and grueling backbreaking farm work. Our voices were often unheard. Boys were valued more than girls. Poverty and limited access to education fueled this systemic marginalization, leaving little room for dreams. Girls were seen as outsiders, expected to marry early and keep the cycle going. The early marriage further restricted opportunities for personal growth and skill development. Despite these formidable obstacles, a yearning for knowledge burned within me. This yearning, coupled with a fierce determination to forge my own path, became the driving force behind my educational journey. It was a path fraught with challenges – navigating societal expectations, overcoming resource limitations, and continuously proving my worth in a system built to favor others.

But with each hurdle cleared, my resolve only strengthened. I devoured every scrap of knowledge I could find, excelling in academics despite the limitations placed upon me. Fueled by a lifelong passion for humanity at a young age, which eventually carved its path, leading me to the noble embrace of a career in healthcare. And when the opportunity arose, it felt less like a choice and more like a resounding answer to a lifelong calling. I was drawn to the nursing profession, a career path that would allow me to serve those in need. In 2003, I obtained my first degree in nursing in Nigeria. That same year, driven by a personal commitment to professional growth, I traveled to the United States.

About four years after my arrival in the United States, I secured a position as a registered charge nurse with the State of New York, Office of Mental Health at the Manhattan Psychiatric Center. Recognizing my potential, the institution later promoted me to a nurse administrator position and facilitated my transfer to the Capital District Psychiatric Center in Albany, NY. While I thrived in my supervisory role, overseeing night shift operations and making critical medical decisions regarding patient care, the financial compensation did not align with the demands of the position. Despite my responsible budgeting, the salary unfortunately proved inadequate, leading me to defer some bills each month.

Car loans became a significant burden, and at a point, we were forced to relinquish one of our vehicles due to our inability to make the payments. For a long period, we struggled to manage with just one car. One particularly harsh winter, I vividly recall the desperate situation of not having heating oil to keep our home warm. With a newborn in the house, we huddled together near the kitchen stove, desperately seeking warmth throughout the long night. The following day, a seemingly miraculous event unfolded. An oil delivery truck unexpectedly arrived in our backyard and filled our empty tank. While we later learned it was a company's error, the immediate relief was undeniable. We were finally warm again, and though repayment took time, our family was granted a much-needed reprieve. This experience solidified my belief in the power of unexpected kindness of God, a form of miracle in its own right.

Financial pressures ultimately led me to resign from my secure state position. I then accepted a role as assistant director of nursing in a famous nursing home. However, my tenure there, lasting only two to three months, became a stark awakening to the harsh realities of racial prejudice. It was a double blow: not only was I informed that I was the first Black person to hold such a position, but my well-intentioned recommendations aimed at improving patient care outcomes were met with resistance. Throughout my career in medicine, my core value has been to make a positive impact on patients' lives. Finding myself ostracized and unable to enact positive change, I felt out of place and ultimately knew this wasn't the environment for me. The decision to resign was clear.

Interestingly, this experience, though disheartening, proved to be a pivotal moment in my career path. Fueled by a renewed sense of purpose and a desire for professional growth, I embarked on a journey to pursue a Bachelor of Science degree in Nursing (BSN). In hindsight, this unexpected turn of events seems to have been divinely orchestrated, leading me down a path that better aligned with my aspirations.

My youngest son (Nathan) wasn't even one year old when I took the plunge and enrolled into the BSN program. I was determined to turn a new page in my life, even if it meant juggling diapers and textbooks. While in school, I simultaneously accepted a supervisory position at a nursing home. The facility, unfortunately, presented a demanding environment that was nearly deplorable. As the sole night supervisor, I was responsible for managing numerous units filled with critically ill patients. The workload was immense, leading not only to burnout, but also to a state of mental, physical, and emotional exhaustion. Stress, anxiety, and depression became constant companions. My nights were spent in a whirlwind of activity – responding to calls from nurses, assessing critically ill patients, and sadly, certifying deaths.

After closing my shift each morning, I would head straight to the library to dedicate time to my studies before returning home. My husband, displaying unwavering support, ensured the children, including our newborn in daycare, were prepared for school. In spite of the immense pressure of caring for four young children, my elderly mother, and a full-time job, I persevered, ultimately graduating with the prestigious honor of summa cum laude.

Faced with the harsh realities of financial strain, I considered a shift in my career path. The world of legal nursing initially appealed to me, particularly the advertised salary. Determined to achieve a better work-life balance and financial security, I pursued this new direction, incurring additional debt for the necessary training. While I diligently completed the course and even participated in out-of-state training and conferences, the reality of the job description diverged from my initial expectations. The prospect of spending hours poring over medical records and acting as an expert witness in court held little appeal for me.

My true calling, I realized, lay in direct patient interaction. I found deep satisfaction in understanding their struggles, offering emotional and psychological support, and providing treatment – a form of care that felt divinely ordained for my skill set. This experience underscored the importance of looking beyond the surface appeal of an opportunity. Life's choices require a nuanced approach; what appears promising may not always be the best fit. Some options, while seemingly attractive, offer limited long-term value. These should be weighed against opportunities that hold greater potential and better align with our goals.

Shortly after completing the legal nurse program, I made the difficult decision to shelve the certificate and pursue travel nursing – a choice driven by immediate financial needs. While this path necessitated a quick transition, my financial situation was precarious. Remaining in my previous role meant minimal income, and without a change, the hardship would only worsen with each passing year, leaving the future uncertain.

The decision to become a travel nurse, while driven by financial necessity, came at a significant personal cost. Leaving my family behind was a constant source of anguish. The constant cycle of relocation presented a multitude of challenges: adapting to new environments, ensuring my safety in unfamiliar places, securing temporary housing, and grappling with the emotional strain of separation from loved ones. Despite these burdens, professionalism remained paramount. I discharged my duties diligently, all the while holding onto the hope of a brighter future – a future where these sacrifices would pave the way for a more secure life for myself and my family.

An unexpected encounter during a travel nursing assignment served as a powerful reminder of the impact nurses can have. While shopping at a Walmart one day, I came face-to-face with a former patient. Though I had forgotten her, she instantly recognized me and expressed her immense gratitude for the care I provided during a difficult period of mental breakdown. The public setting added a layer of curiosity, as our racial backgrounds differed. Her heartfelt words resonated deeply: "You were there for me when there was no hope and everything seemed dark. Please continue to help the helpless and those in hopeless situations like I was." This emotional encounter filled me with a profound sense of fulfillment. It reignited my passion for helping others and served as a powerful source of resilience, propelling me forward in my chosen career.

Financial security undeniably plays a crucial role in a fulfilling life, enabling a comfortable lifestyle and supporting loved ones. However, pursuing a career you find intrinsically rewarding is the ultimate key to true fulfillment.

A Crossroads of Challenges and Miracles: A Doctor's Tale

> During one of the travel nursing assignments, I experienced a pivotal moment. I felt a calling, a gentle nudge from within, urging me to take the next step in my professional development – pursuing a graduate program. While some I confided in expressed reservations, my husband, with unwavering support, readily endorsed this new chapter.
>
> I submitted applications to three universities, and paid the associated fees. Fortunately, I received acceptance letters from all of them. However, the decision of which one to attend remained. While I contemplated

my options, I received a strong internal prompting that none of these schools were the right fit. As a human being, I questioned the legitimacy of the voice I heard. Nevertheless, because of my past experiences with God's guidance through the Holy Spirit, I made the difficult decision to decline admission to all three universities, forfeiting the application fees I had paid.

Then there was a prompt to consider State University at Buffalo, New York, a six-hour drive from my home. Upon researching the program at the University of Buffalo, I discovered that only two weeks remained before the application deadline. This presented a significant challenge, as the program required the MAT exam, which typically necessitates at least three months of preparation and boasts an average passing score of 400. Remarkably, I managed to complete the lengthy application process, pass the MAT exam within the limited timeframe, and secure an interview with a panel of professors.

Despite lacking formal interview preparation and possessing limited knowledge of the interview format, I instinctively turned to prayer. Following the guidance of our pastor, I implored God to favor me. Remarkably, the interview consisted of only one question, with the remaining time dedicated to a discussion of my family background and career path.

The interview concluded with a surprising revelation from the interviewers. They had stated that due to the rigorous nature of the program, and the demanding commitment, it was typically intended for residents of Western New York, who could be physically present on campus throughout the program. Additionally, the professors explained that notification of admissions decisions typically takes three weeks.

To my astonishment, my situation unfolded differently. Not only was I granted immediate admission, the professors individually welcomed and congratulated me. The unexpected enthusiasm that filled the room left me stunned. This experience solidified my belief that I was guided by God's grace and headed in the right direction.

I shared the news of my acceptance with my spiritual mentors, Pastors Lanre and Abiola Peters. They responded with fervent prayer and offered their unwavering support, both in tangible ways and through spiritual guidance. The logistical challenges of relocating to Buffalo, particularly without my family accompanying me initially, became readily apparent. My son was only two years old at the time. We embarked on a weeks-long search for suitable housing, ultimately settling on an option that significantly depleted our financial resources.

Parting with my family was a tearful affair. Hugs and kisses were exchanged as I drove away, my vision blurred by tears. As I navigated the I-95 highway, a torrent of emotions overwhelmed me. Questions swirled in my mind: "Was this the right decision? What would become of my children and husband? What if I failed? How would I manage the six-hour commute between Albany and Buffalo for more than four years? Could this lead to marital strain? Could the stress of my situation trigger health problems?" These, and countless other anxieties, flooded my thoughts.

My graduate studies, encompassing both my master's and doctoral degrees, proved to be the most demanding experience of my life. The journey challenged me on a spiritual, emotional, and intellectual level. At a time, I succumbed to depression and contemplated abandoning my studies. However, whenever I felt the urge to quit, my husband and pastors, Lanre and Abiola Peters, would unfailingly intervene, offering resolute encouragement with the words "you can do this, we've got your back." Their steadfast support proved true in every sense. My husband, in particular, made significant personal sacrifices, exceeding his own limitations to ensure the success of my academic journey.

My pastors played a multifaceted role in supporting my family during my academic years. Their contributions ranged from offering prayers and encouragement to providing invaluable therapeutic guidance and counsel. One particular instance stands out in my memory. Pastor Abiola called to check on me, approximately three weeks into the program. At that time, I was overwhelmed by a sense of confusion. Unsure of how to navigate the classroom environment or interact with others, I felt isolated. Notably, I was one of the two Black students in the program, and the only one who identified as African. Additionally, I found myself as the oldest student in most of my classes, even older than some of my professors.

My attempts to mingle and seek guidance on navigating the coursework proved unsuccessful. Every effort yielded generic responses that failed to address my specific challenges. Discouraged, I was in my apartment when Pastor Abiola's call came in again. Her inquiry about my well-being was a welcome intervention. She then offered a powerful statement: "Sister Patricia, you must not question why you took this step. Never regret your decision" While I expressed gratitude, internally, I acknowledged the numerous times I had both questioned and regretted my choice. Pastor Abiola then provided both prayer and prophetic words, leaving me feeling significantly more encouraged.

Following this conversation with Pastor Abiola, I experienced a profound spiritual realization. I felt the Holy Spirit prompting me, "You are seeking assistance from humans who are limited in their ability to help. Do not forget the One who brought you here." This revelation led me to kneel in prayer, seeking forgiveness and guidance. Almost instantaneously, I received an intuitive understanding of the coursework.

From that point forward, my studies progressed remarkably. Undeterred by the demands of motherhood (four children!), being a wife, and managing the challenges of being an older student of color, I persevered.

The support from my family, friends, and spiritual mentors was my lifeline, pulling me up when I stumbled, reminding me why I started climbing in the first place. With the firm support of my husband I knew I wouldn't be alone on the summit. With all the support by my side, the whispers of doubt faded, replaced by a quiet hum of determination. Although I still had tough days, tears still stained my textbooks, but I never let go of that tiny spark of hope that helped me keep burning. This wasn't just about a degree; it was about proving to myself, and maybe a little to the doubts, that I could conquer this academic *Everest*. Not only did I persevere till the end, I never failed or repeated any course, and I graduated with distinctions.

From Witness to a Healer: My Career in Mental Health

My interest in mental health can be traced back to the early 1980s, a time sparked by the chilling experiences I witnessed in my own community. Opposite my father's house lay a compound, where the owner, under the guise of treatment, housed and subjected individuals with mental illness to unspeakable horrors. As a young girl, I naively joined other children in observing these people, who were cruelly labeled "mad people". The "healer" was a traditional herbalist who relied solely on herbal remedies.

Unfortunately, many families, desperate to avoid the stigma and public shame associated with mental illness, had limited options. In a misguided attempt to shield their loved ones from public scrutiny, they entrusted them to this herbalist, who lacked both formal education and any understanding of mental illness. He exploited the vulnerability of these unfortunate people for his own gain.

The individuals with mental illness were considered outcasts, demon possessed, and ostracized by a community too quick to judge and too afraid to understand. The humiliation, the maltreatment, the soul-crushing abuse carved scars not just on their flesh but on my own young heart. The "healer's" methods were barbaric. Patients deemed mentally ill were bound to trees with chains, subjected to beatings with a cane each morning, and then forced to consume herbal concoctions. The aftermath was chilling – a zombie-like state followed by a period of sleep. I have no recollection of them receiving food or water beyond these herbs. As a young girl, I was deeply troubled by the inhumane treatment of these individuals. The trauma of witnessing this ignited a passion within me to delve deeper into the root causes of mental illness.

While the science of mental illness was far less developed in my community then, it's clear that biological and genetic factors likely played a significant role in the struggles of those I witnessed. Unfortunately, at that time, there were limited means of diagnosis or intervention. This experience, however, sparked a deep curiosity within me. As I transitioned into the modern world, I was drawn to pursue a career in psychiatry, driven by a desire to understand the brain and its connection to mental illness. Also, driven by a desire to expand my knowledge base and effectively address the diverse needs of my patients with mental health challenges, I pursued a doctoral degree. This not only bolstered my professional confidence but also equipped me with autonomy and a broader perspective on the disease process. I now possess a deeper understanding of my patients' needs that extends beyond their diagnoses. I now recognize how psychosocial factors contribute to mental illness and how significantly it can impact treatment outcomes.

The urge to go back to my village and serve the community that first ignited my passion remains strong but unfortunately, the opportunity was cruelly snatched away by unforeseen circumstances, including devastating tribal wars that displaced many from the region. Yet, the spirit of service remained undimmed. Here in the United States, I found and engaged with a new community in need, an underserved population of individuals grappling with mental health and addiction challenges. In their eyes, I see echoes of my own people, and in their struggles, a reflection of the journey that first set me on this path.

The adage "nothing good comes easy" resonates deeply with my experience. My educational and professional journey has emphasized the importance of sacrifice in achieving goals. My four-year plus educational voyage with a six-hour commute between Albany and Buffalo, a 600-mile round trip, demanded steady dedication. Winter storms, fog, and exhaustion all presented challenges. There were instances where I struggled to stay awake at the steering of my car, unintentionally drifting lanes. However, I am grateful for the grace of God that protected me throughout those journeys. His benevolence extended beyond me, safeguarding my family and providing encouragement to my husband and children during those demanding years.

My perseverance bore fruit, as I became one of the first in my generation to earn a doctorate degree in my chosen profession, an accomplishment I know could only come from divine blessing. This accomplishment stands as an attestation to God's grace and mercy. This is not just a career; it is a calling. It is a witness to the enduring power of human resilience, a bridge between the shadows of the past and the promise of a brighter future. And as I walk alongside individuals with mental illness, offering solace and support, I know that the seeds of hope I sow today will blossom into a healthier, more compassionate world for all.

As I turn the page on this chapter, my heart overflows

with gratitude for God's boundless divine intervention. He shielded me from harms and potential accidents, granting me a second chance to fulfill my purpose on Earth.

CHAPTER 9: MY PHILANTHROPIC MISSION

My upbringing took place in an underserved community, where adults and children alike labored together to secure a livelihood. The concept of proper nutrition or adequate nourishment remained elusive for many children. Access to clean drinking water, healthcare, education, and even basic necessities were severely limited. Our homes were typically constructed with thatched roofs and mud walls. Remarkably, despite these significant challenges, the community fostered a strong sense of harmony. A sense of community and shared experience fostered contentment. Although we were unaware of a different, potentially better life beyond our circumstances then, the strong sense of belonging encouraged happiness even amidst our impoverishment.

The harsh realities of our situation became tragically evident when I was eight years old. My beloved baby sister caved in to an unknown illness. The absence of formal medical infrastructures and qualified personnels meant there was no way to diagnose her condition. My father, in desperation, turned to a traditional healer, believed to possess supernatural powers for healing and manipulating spirits. Sadly, despite rituals, incantations, and sacrifices, my sister passed away. The cause of her death remains unknown to this day.

My childhood in an impoverished community provided me with firsthand experience of poverty. This tragedy, etched in my childhood, became a stark lesson in the crippling grip of poverty. Witnessing my family's vulnerability, our lack of access to basic needs and healthcare, instilled in me a profound understanding of how socioeconomic status, environment, and education shape life's trajectory and well-being. It laid bare the brutal reality of how poverty batters not just individuals, but entire communities. It showed me the strength of a community, the resilience of the human spirit, and the importance of never to take anything for granted. My life experience sparked a fire in me, a mission to make a difference, to ensure others wouldn't have to face the same hardships I did. That's my philanthropic mission, born from the dust and straw of an unlikely paradise.

Those challenges, struggles, and obstacles I faced throughout my life, compelled me to give back to the less fortunate in my Nigerian community. In 2019, my husband and I established a non-profit foundation in Nigeria to reach out to individuals facing life's difficulties. Inspired by our own faith journey, we named the foundation "Grace for Grace International Foundation," reflecting the biblical principle in John 1:16 *Amplified Bible, Classic Edition* (AMPC): "For out of His fullness (abundance) we have all received [all had a share and we were all supplied with] one grace after another and spiritual blessing upon spiritual blessing and even favor upon favor and gift [heaped] upon gift." This bountiful grace, generously bestowed upon us, now flows outward, enriching the lives of countless others.

Our foundation, guided by the motto "Service to

Humanity," strives to bring hope to the despondent and reignite the spirits of those who have lost sight of life's possibilities. Our mission finds profound inspiration in Isaiah 41:13 *New International Version* (NIV): "For I the Lord your God hold your right hand; it is I who say to you, 'Fear not, I will help you"

Since its inception, the foundation has operated independently, relying on the founders' contributions. However, in 2021, following a partnership request from the General Overseer of the Chosen Race Assembly of Praise in Abakaliki, Ebonyi State, Nigeria, the foundation provided financial support for a targeted relief effort. This initiative distributed essential supplies (palliatives) to vulnerable members of the community, widows from various parts of the community, internally displaced individuals, and victims of the Eza/Effiom communal war. Cooked meals and drinks were served on-site, while staple goods like bags of rice, noodles, and assorted condiments were provided for ongoing needs.

Beyond this specific partnership, the foundation has consistently supported disadvantaged children by helping them pursue their education. It has also empowered families by launching small businesses and provided crucial housing assistance to widows.

We believe that access to education empowers individuals to break the cycle of poverty that has impacted their families for generations. Education equips people with the skills and knowledge to secure gainful employment, leading to a more productive and fulfilling life.

For us, every smile, every child sent to school, and every family thriving in their own business, is a testament to the power of compassion and God's grace. We are not just offering a helping hand; we are building a bridge to a brighter future, one act of service at a time. Nonetheless, our efforts, while crucial, represent only one piece of the puzzle. To truly alleviate poverty on a societal level, a systemic approach is necessary. We must address the root causes of poverty, not just to provide temporary relief. And this is where advocacy becomes essential.

I firmly believe that advocating for the underprivileged can lead to policy changes that promote equity and opportunity. These policies can dismantle the complex web of factors that perpetuate social inequality. With steady faith and the support of generous individuals, we can collectively make a significant difference in people's lives.

The foundation is committed to continuous improvement in its philanthropic efforts. One long-term goal is to establish a sustainable water system for the village, once the tribal conflict has subsided. Additionally, we aim to build a medical center that provides treatment for individuals with mental illness in a judgment free zone.

These are just glimpses of the bigger picture we're striving to paint. We believe that with consistent advocacy, strategic interventions, and unfaltering compassion, we can chip away the roots of poverty and build a brighter future for generations to come.

Imagine an equitable society where everyone has a fair shot at a decent life, free from the shackles of economic disparity. That's the dream that fuels my passion for advocacy.

But it's not a solo journey, I believe in the power of collaboration, in joining hands with fellow "Good

Samaritans" (love that term!) to create a collective impact. That's why our foundation, *Grace for Grace International*, actively seeks partnerships and donations to amplify our reach and effectiveness.

The Scripture teaches us of God's deep compassion for the poor. This concern is evident throughout the Bible, with clear calls to action for God's followers. The Mosaic Law exemplifies this principle, establishing mechanisms to care for the underprivileged. For instance, Leviticus 19:9-10 instructs the Israelites not to harvest all their grapes; they were ordered to leave some for the poor and foreigners residing among them.

The New Testament reinforces this message. In James 1:27, apostle James defines pure religion as caring for orphans and widows in their suffering. Poverty has been a persistent challenge throughout human history, and it likely will continue to exist as long as social and economic hierarchies remain. While the problem may seem daunting, it doesn't negate our responsibility to help.

Helping those in need should be a selfless act, driven by a genuine desire to make a positive impact. Fortunately, creating meaningful change doesn't require grand gestures. Even small contributions, like offering spare change, your time, a shared meal, or clothing donations, can make a significant difference. Many mistakenly believe that helping requires vast resources, but that's simply not true. Any act of charity, however small, has the potential to improve another person's life. No matter how insignificant your kind gesture may feel, it holds the power to create positive change.

Charitable acts, while essential for raising living standards, don't eliminate the wide gap between the wealthy and the poor entirely. However, they do play a crucial role in narrowing the gap. My faith teaches me that sharing with the less fortunate is an act of faith, trust, and belief in God's providence, as exemplified in John 3:16. God's ultimate gift, Jesus Christ, embodies the concept of giving out of love to meet human needs. By extending a helping hand to those in poverty, we strengthen our own faith in God's provision, acknowledge His Lordship over our resources, and deepen our trust in Him. The act of giving also offers long-lasting physical and psychological benefits to the recipients themselves.

Life experiences have a funny way of shaking our complacency. Getting stuck in our own "bubbles" often breeds tunnel vision, amplifying our own struggles and blinding us to the needs of others. But when we reach out to those in need, the world suddenly comes into sharper focus. When we become overly focused on our own problems and struggles, we lose sight of the suffering of others. Helping those in need has shifted my perspective. Now, I find myself expressing gratitude for my blessings rather than dwelling on what I lack.

Before I exit this chapter, I'd like to offer some practical tips on getting involved in giving back. Don't wait until you have immense wealth – start with empathy. Try to see the world through the eyes of those in need, understand their struggles, and recognize our shared humanity.

There are many ways to contribute. You can support existing organizations by donating money, food, clothing, or your valuable time. Even a listening ear and a kind word can be immensely helpful to someone facing hardship. A simple gesture of compassion can brighten someone's day and offer them a renewed sense of hope. As a renowned philanthropist once said, "What makes us human is not the ability to think but the ability to love." When you give with kindness and compassion, you are truly making a positive difference in the world.

So, offer the kind of love you yourself would yearn for. Let your compassion guide your actions, whether it's a generous donation, a dedicated volunteer shift, or just a moment of genuine connection. Believe me, every act of giving, big or small, ripples outwards, paving the way for a brighter future for all.

CHAPTER 10: THE EMERGENCE OF A STAR BABY

Growing up, the adage "never say never" was engraved in my teenage mind. Little did I know, it would become a mantra echoed in the most unexpected chapter of my life. When we welcomed our fourth child, a rambunctious boy (Nathan), at the ripe age of 40, our desire for the "perfect" family of three had already been surpassed. This unexpected arrival, prompted by a revelation my husband experienced, stretched our limits. Juggling four kids, careers, and finances felt like a constant sprint.

Relief finally washed over us as our second son transitioned to kindergarten. We celebrated our escape from the diaper world; dreaming of family portraits that remained uncaptured even now. Our prayers for financial security intensified, fueled by the desire to grant our children the opportunities we never had. With my doctorate in hand, I dove into planning of projects, events, and travel, blissfully unaware of the surprise lurking just around the corner.

Nine years had passed since my last farewell to the delivery room. Then the unexpected unfolded. It all began with the astonishing vision that I had given birth to a baby who not only emerged but immediately stood up and spoke. When my husband relayed this incredible revelation, I initially dismissed it with laughter. Curiosity piqued, I couldn't help but ask, "Why are you always the one to receive these revelations? Why wasn't I granted this knowledge beforehand, so I could have a say?

As I grappled with the revelation, humorously dismissing it with comments like "there's no need for another Jesus" and questioning the possibility of pregnancy at my age, a seed had quietly taken root within me. Before I could even formulate proper questions for God, and before my doubts found voice, the seed had begun to grow.

A torrent of questions flooded my mind as I began to tussle with this new reality. "God, what purpose could this serve?" I cried out inwardly. "Is this part of the double blessing we've been praying for?" I quickly dismissed the notion. "You know how much we're struggling financially, Lord," I pleaded. "We desperately need a breakthrough, yet you offer me...pregnancy?"

Caught in this bewilderment, I questioned my own sanity, "Am I dreaming?" the thought echoed in my head. The only answer that came back was a silent, disbelieving echo: "No way, this must be a joke." For a few weeks, I was locked in a constant internal debate. The same questions swirled around in my mind, unanswered, a frustrating loop with no resolution.

In a desperate attempt to shield myself from the overwhelming emotions, I convinced myself that these were simply symptoms of approaching menopause, after all, my 50th birthday loomed just a few months away. I clung to this explanation, voicing my pleas to God. "Please", I implored, "let this cup pass me by". "If this truly was a child", I offered, "please give it to the young couples in our church longing for children." In a moment of desperation,

I even made a vow: "God, if you set me free from this, I'll be more careful, or better yet, I'll abstain from intimacy altogether. Surely, after twenty years, we've had enough." But my pleas seemed to fall on deaf ears. The more fervently I ranted, the deeper the silence from above.

Five weeks passed, an agonizing wait for my period's mysterious return, nothing happened. Reality dawned: I was in for a bigger surprise than I anticipated. Desperate for confirmation, I confided in the medical director I worked with. She readily entertained the possibility of menopause-related symptoms, a diagnosis I clung to, unwilling to face the truth nature was offering, as I wasn't ready to accept it. But despite my mental resistance, relaxation proved elusive. The more I tried to quiet my mind, the more my body betrayed me, a constant hum of discomfort growing steadily.

Weeks of denial and panic culminated, my husband, the visionary, urged me to take a pregnancy test. **Driven by both trepidation and a flicker of hope, I rushed to the nearest Walgreens store,** and grabbed a kit. Before the test strip could even fully absorb the sample, the result flashed back, "Pregnant". Disbelief clouded my vision. "Were my glasses dirty?" I wiped them frantically, rereading the result – still pregnant. Washing my face didn't change the reality staring back at me. Another test the next day yielded the same answer.

A fever of unknown origin suddenly gripped me. Sweating, shivering, and utterly confused, I embarked on another round of internal dialogue. "Is this a dream? Am I even awake?", I'd mutter, punctuated by bursts of strange laughter – a reaction uncomfortably similar to what's known as labile affect in a mental health condition called schizophrenia.

My erratic behavior continued until my dreamer husband intervened. He urged me to stop fretting about God's blessings, and then surprised me with a seemingly confessional statement. "Back in Nigeria," he admitted, I foolishly told God I wanted six children. "Do you remember the saying about the power of words?", I asked.

His voice held a hint of sheepishness: "I know," he conceded, "but even covenants can be broken. I've already asked God to put a stop to it – I have enough on my plate as it is." Disappointment washed over me at first, but the deep love we shared acted as a shield, preventing further escalation. However, his confession sent me reeling. A thick fog clouded my mind, leaving me numb and unable to process the future.

As a devout Christian, abortion was unthinkable, and every child given by God is for a divine purpose. But how could I possibly embark on this journey again? My eldest child would be turning twenty in just a few months, an age when I might already be a grandparent, had life unfolded differently. The weight of it all pressed down on me, leading me to a startling conclusion: perhaps a supernatural force was guiding my life in an extraordinary way.

The relentless morning sickness forced me to abandon church services. However, as fate would have it, Pastor Lanre Peters, known for his attentiveness, called to check on me after two missed Sundays. Seizing the opportunity, I confessed my situation. After a few startled "Jesus!" exclamations, Pastor Peters launched into a prophecy.

"Dr. Patricia, he boomed, this is a message! God truly loves you. At fifty! Many young people out there crave such a blessing. If God has chosen you for this assignment, we should give Him thanks!" He then offered a prayer for strength and grace, to which I wholeheartedly echoed, "Amen!" Pastor Peters' words were a balm to my soul. As I pondered upon them, it dawned on me: yes, this must be a message to the world. Age or science for Christians, cannot dictate the hand of God.

Pastor Abiola Peters' call the next day brought a much-needed boost to my spirits. Her encouraging words not only lifted my mood but also led me to a deeper understanding of the spiritual side of things. Concluding our first conversation, she declared, "That's a baby on a mission, Dr. Patricia. God has a message for the world, and He wants you to deliver it!" Following our talk, she sent me a book titled "Prayer and Confessions During Pregnancy" by Dayo Dosumu. Curiosity kindled as I devoured the pages, searching for stories that mirrored my situation. However, the author's focus was on maintaining strength and offering positive affirmations to your unborn child. I continued the practice of confession, yet doubt and overwhelm occasionally crept in, reducing me to tears. But then I'd remember: who was I to question God's plan?

Believe it or not, this baby's pregnancy wasn't a result of negligence. For the past nine years, my husband and I have faithfully practiced birth control. Yet, here we are. As Pastor Abiola wisely pointed out, this must be part of my life's journey, and I find myself inclined to agree. Had I written this memoir in 2018, when it was laid in my heart, this extraordinary chapter of my life wouldn't have been included.

Despite my deep depression about the pregnancy, I clung

to my faith, attending weekly Bible studies and occasional prayer meetings. During a particular timely Bible study led by Pastor Abiola, I received an invaluable Rhema – a divinely inspired word – that resonated deeply with my situation.

"Instead of allowing your circumstances to control you", Pastor Abiola declared, "turn them around to your advantage!"

This message became my mantra. I shifted my mindset, embracing positivity. I determined that this unexpected blessing would ultimately strengthen and empower me, not weaken me. With renewed vigor, I tackled my pre-planned activities and even surpassed my own expectations.

My First Prenatal Visit

My first prenatal visit, scheduled for October 13th, 2023, held immense significance. The days leading up to it were marked by a relentless barrage of symptoms – chills, nausea, headaches, fatigue, and a constant battle with vomiting. Due to my medical background, I took a leap of faith and visited the pharmacy, stocking up on prenatal vitamins until my official appointment.

As the date approached, a sliver of hope remained that the sonographer might offer a different diagnosis. However, that hope was swiftly extinguished. The kind woman, beaming with joy, offered her congratulations."You are chosen by God for this assignment," she declared. I have worked in ultrasound for over thirty years, witnessing countless struggles with infertility at all ages. If God has blessed you with pregnancy at this stage, there must be a purpose. He is trying to show us something. Her voice softened further, "I'll be keeping you in my prayers, dear."

The sonographer's words mirrored those of my pastors exactly. This uncanny coincidence solidified my belief that it was a message from above. A few days later, I found myself at LabCorp for my first blood work. As I waited, the phlebotomist drawing my blood inquired about my age. "It's right there on the slip," I replied, pointing. Her response was a burst of laughter.

God doesn't make mistakes, she declared, her voice filled with conviction. She then confided in me about her 35-year-old daughter's struggles with infertility. "You've given me renewed hope", she continued, her eyes shining. "This is a sign that I can still trust in God's plan. There is hope for my daughter too!" In a whirlwind of emotions, she scribbled her name and number on a piece of paper. "Please", she pleaded, "invite me to your baby shower!"

The third message arrived during a conversation with a friend. She shared the story of her 47-year-old niece, married for fifteen years, who still faithfully trusts God for a child. My friend, echoing the sentiment of others, believed God doesn't make mistakes and that every child born is destined for a purpose. Filled with renewed hope, she declared her belief that God would soon bless her niece with the same miracle.

In that moment, a conviction settled within me: this truly was a baby on a mission. As prophesied, the message seemed to be radiating outward, even before the baby's arrival. People were already finding encouragement and hope in my story.

Announcing The New Addition

The time had come to share the news with the kids. My husband called a family meeting. He'd thoughtfully ordered their favorite meal and drinks, setting a relaxed atmosphere. After a brief prayer asking for God's guidance in this delicate conversation, he found himself at a loss for words. With a smile in my direction, he gently passed the baton to me.

Taking a deep breath, I announced, "We are having a new baby!" A stunned silence followed, punctuated only by wide-eyed stares. It seemed like a full minute passed before the dam broke.

Our youngest, Nathan, launched into a barrage of questions. "Is it a boy? When's the baby coming?" His excitement bubbled over. A few minutes later, Nathan reappeared, his face beaming with uncontainable joy. He practically vibrated with excitement as he announced, launching into a heartfelt confession. "I'm so glad I won't be the last-born anymore! Do you guys know how annoying it is to always be bossed around by older siblings? I get to be a big brother now! I will have someone to look up to me! I've been praying for a younger sibling for ages!" He punctuated his declaration with a burst of celebratory breakdancing.

My husband and I were speechless, watching him express himself so openly. Finally, I managed a simple, "Congratulations, Nathan, your prayers have been answered." This outburst of joy took on a new significance in light of Nathan's recent behavior. He'd been uncharacteristically moody and withdrawn for a while. Now, it seemed his prayers had not only been answered for a sibling, but also for a release from whatever had been troubling him.

As a mental health expert, I'm naturally attuned to people's behavior. Prior to the pregnancy announcement, I'd tried on several occasions to understand what was troubling him. While he'd always insist he was "fine", the news of the baby sparked a remarkable shift in his mood. Since then, he's been in a state of constant elation, unusually happy. He became incredibly invested in the pregnancy's progress, bombarding me with questions several times a day. "Is the baby kicking?", he'd ask, keeping meticulous track of the weeks, both past and present. He diligently monitored my vitamin intake, constantly reminding me, and expressing his joy with a cheerful, "We're making progress!"

Our ten-year-old son (Aaron) , ever the pragmatist, piped up, "Dad, I thought this meeting was about winning the lottery!" A beat of surprised silence followed before he added, with a grin, "Well, guess, you won something even better – a pregnancy!" The unexpected comment sent ripples of laughter through the room, catching everyone off guard.

Our twelve-year-old daughter's reaction was a mix of surprise and pragmatism. "Wow, I wasn't expecting this at all," she admitted. "It's been eight years, so I kind of figured...well, never mind. I just hope it's a girl!" With a playful jab, she added, "Please no more visions, I can't afford to have six siblings".

Our nineteen-year-old daughter, embracing her role as the big sister, showered me with constant encouragement. She'd call regularly from school to check in, her voice brimming with excitement. In her eyes, this new arrival was undoubtedly a gift from God. By the end of the family meeting, everyone was in agreement: the baby was indeed a blessing, a special gift from God.

The excitement was contagious. The kids, united in purpose, immediately embarked on a mission to find names that reflected this divine gift. The boys scoured lists of male names, while the girls delved into the world of feminine choices. Eagerly, they voted for the tie breaker. Now, all that remained was the joyful anticipation of the baby's gender reveal.

My initial apprehension about the pregnancy gradually transformed. As my thoughts and feelings evolved, I began to view it as a remarkable undertaking. Determined to succeed, I embraced diligence, patience, and perseverance. This journey of faith, destined to be a cherished memory, inspired me to document this pivotal moment in my life. Hence, the existence of this excerpt.

Prayer became my anchor during this challenging time. I sought strength to navigate each day and favor from my workplace. Thankfully, my prayers were answered. The medical director proved to be an exceptional source of support, offering not only her expertise but also her kindness. She even went the extra mile by preparing Indian food for me – a thoughtful gesture that went a long way in boosting my morale. The overall director was equally reassuring, making a point to stop by my office daily to inquire about my well-being. The manager was not left out.

The support extended beyond leadership. The nurses and clinicians were incredibly helpful. One of the older nurses, assuming a motherly role, brought me a variety of foods and even provided a portable heater to combat the chills.

The constant battle with excessive saliva presented its own set of challenges. Confined to my office, I struggled to have even brief conversations without resorting to discreet spitting. Even wearing a face mask when others didn't felt insufficient. Attending to patients in the exam room while battling this discomfort was particularly mortifying, often requiring me to excuse myself several times. Despite these obstacles, I maintained my composure with my patients, refusing to let hormonal fluctuations compromise my professionalism.

The Big Gender Reveal

The long-awaited moment finally arrived after our second prenatal appointment. This time, I underwent a blood test to definitively determine the baby's gender. The suspense was palpable! As I left the hospital that day, the midwife, with a playful smile, handed me a sealed envelope. "Why don't you and your husband open this together in front of the kids?", she suggested.

As usual, we gathered the family for a meeting. Nathan who'd been faithfully praying for a sibling, was given the honor of opening the envelope. Curiosity etched on his face, he tore the envelope open with a flourish, "It's a girl!!!!!", he shrieked, his voice laced with excitement. Then, with a burst of exuberance that defied gender preference, he launched into another dance, clearly thrilled about the prospect of becoming a big brother, not minding the gender.

His older brother, however, couldn't hide a touch of disappointment – his heart set on a little brother. But the girls, ecstatic to have won the "sibling gender tie-breaker," erupted in cheers.

Nathan remained deeply invested in the pregnancy.

He spent a good chunk of time watching YouTube videos on baby care, eagerly learning how to feed and entertain his soon-to-be baby sister. His enthusiasm was infectious; he'd constantly ask if I'd shared the news with everyone, from friends to church members. Witnessing Nathan's joy, my husband remarked one day, "Perhaps God orchestrated this not just for us, but to save a soul. Who knows what would have happened without this pregnancy."

High-Risk Pregnancies

Pregnancy is considered to be high-risk for mothers under 18 and over 35. For women over 45, pregnancy becomes uncommon and carries a greater chance of complications for both mother and baby. These complications can include miscarriage, stillbirth, high blood pressure (hypertension), gestational diabetes, preeclampsia, a rare form of cancer called gestational trophoblastic disease, and chromosomal abnormalities like Down Syndrome.

Medically, I have all the risk factors associated with high risk pregnancy: first, I am an African American, my age, gender, and pre-pregnancy overweight.

Despite these documented risks, I was fortunate to experience a healthy pregnancy, free of complications. My blood pressure even remained lower than before pregnancy, and all my lab tests came back normal. I credit this to the divine intervention of God, whose blessings were evident throughout the pregnancy journey. Thankfully, I required no medication beyond prenatal vitamins, not even common pain relievers like Tylenol.

Our journey reached a joyful climax with the much-anticipated arrival of our precious daughter. Originally, her due date was estimated for mid-May of this year. However, during a routine prenatal checkup in April, I received some unexpected news.

My doctor recommended immediate delivery due to concerns about the baby's health. I was instructed to go to the labor ward and told the baby will be delivered within two hours. This came as a complete surprise, as I had been eagerly anticipating her arrival on the expected date of birth, and carefully counting down the days and weeks.

The news sent a jolt through me. A wave of fear, panic, and anxiety washed over me. My heart hammered in my chest, and tremors wracked my body.

The following hours were a blur of medical intervention. Needles pricked my veins for intravenous fluids, while others numbed my lower body for anesthesia. Fear gripped me, and the only clear memory I have is of praying fervently, asking God to guide their hands and ensure my safety.

Thankfully, with my husband by my side and the skilled medical team present, divine providence intervened. Within thirty to sixty minutes, a healthy cry announced the arrival of my baby girl. A wave of relief engulfed me as I weakly whispered, "I'm still here," followed by a heartfelt, "Thank you, Jesus." This episode concludes the saying, "man proposes but God disposes"

The First Weeks: Challenges and Triumphs

While the pregnancy journey was successful without any complications, the initial weeks of postpartum presented a multitude of challenges. I wrestled with pain, bleeding, general discomfort, limited mobility, and high blood pressure. Despite these difficulties, a powerful mix of excitement and apprehension colored my experience. Through it all, I found strength and resilience, emerging victorious.

Welcoming Baby Nwaefuna

The elation that washes over one after the ordeal of childbirth is truly profound. Gazing upon a newborn child, a perfect gift from God, one cannot help but marvel at the miracle of creation.

Great thinkers have long considered the human body a temple of mystery. Yet, witnessing the arrival of a child, a flawless image of God's love, solidifies the concept of a divine miracle. In a mere span of months, a new life comes into existence, a testament to the magnificence, worth, beauty, and grandeur inherent in God's infinite perfection.

Our family is brimming with excitement as we welcome our precious child, Chinwe (God's own), Lael (belonging to God), Uchechukwu (God's will),Theresa (harvest) Nwaefuna. Our prayers for her are filled with hope for God's guidance, wisdom, protection, and strength as she embarks on her earthly journey, fulfilling her unique purpose in this world.

EPILOGUE

Reclaiming Purpose at the Hands of Providence

Life is a mystical journey that unfolds along a winding path filled with peaks of joy, and valleys of despair. The highway of life, as I've come to know it, is anything but a smooth, predictable tarmac. It meanders through sun-drenched meadows and storm-wracked valleys, offering up moments of unbridled joy that echo through childhood streets and memories that shimmer like fireflies in the twilight of my mind. We all experience moments of celebration and cherished memories, balanced by the inevitable anguish and challenges that life throws our way. Yet, it is through these very wonders, both joyous and difficult, that we shape our destinies.

But within this intricate dance of light and shadow, I've discovered a profound truth: life is not a problem to be solved, nor a puzzle to be deciphered. It is an adventure, a magnificent mystery unfolding before our very eyes. Each twist and turn, whether meticulously planned or unintentionally stumbled upon, shapes our purpose and defines our essence.

To navigate this odyssey with grace and truly claim victory over its inevitable trials, we must embrace its entirety. We must accept the shadows of the past, not with regret, but with understanding. We must savor the sweetness of the present, finding gratitude in the simplest of moments.

And, above all, we must face the unknown future with unwavering hope, for it is in the embrace of possibility that our greatest triumphs await.

For many years, I wandered through life adrift, seeking validation in the fleeting echoes of others' approval. My existence before this pivotal journey was but a hollow echo, devoid of purpose and guided by the fickle compass of external acceptance. My spiritual awakening was yet to bloom, its seeds dormant until I grasped the futility of searching for happiness in the ephemeral landscapes of human validation. Then, in a transformative epiphany, I recognized the divine source of true fulfillment – God.

This realization set me on a course of spiritual exploration, a winding path that has stretched across five decades. With each step, I have peeled back layers of self-doubt and embraced the profound wisdom that life is not a destination, but an odyssey of continual growth and discovery.

They say a wish is just a dandelion seed drifting on the wind, pretty but fragile. My dreams, though, were rockets fueled by ambition. I wasn't just aiming for stars; I wanted to build constellations. Maybe that's because life hadn't exactly been an "easy street" for me.

I wasn't born with a silver spoon, but I had a fistful of grit and a heart overflowing with talent. It wasn't always easy, it was like climbing a mountain made of broken glass, but I never stopped pushing. Every step, every struggle, was a rung on the ladder to my dreams. My childhood was rougher than sandpaper, but it never snuffed out my spark. Instead, it became the flint against which I sharpened my determination. My journey embodies the essence of the

American Dream – a testament to the indomitable spirit that resides within us all. If I, with nothing but grace as my compass, could navigate such a path, then so can you. Believe, and let that belief guide your own ascent.

The fundamental truth of life is that nothing occurs by happenstance. Grasping this principle ignites introspection, a reflection on the very nature of our existence. As individuals, we are as distinct as the paths we forge. Each journey unfolds with its own unique experiences and destinations.

Years of experience instilled in me the belief that every circumstance carries a divine message. I have learned over the years to listen to the whispers of God in every storm. It was here, amidst the tempestuous waves of experience, that I discovered the chasm between human wisdom and divine orchestration. As Proverbs 19:21 so aptly declares, "Many are the plans in the mind of a man, but it is the purpose of the LORD that will stand."

Who could have foreseen, at the threshold of fifty, that I would be chosen once more to become a vessel for God's message, an instrument to usher in another facet of His legacy? The good news is that, despite the inevitable trepidation, I surrendered to the call, obedient to the very end. Even when I unknowingly pursued earthly ambitions, charted my own course through a multitude of self-made projects, the divine intervention arrived at precisely the opportune moment.

This assignment of childbirth at fifty, though testing the limits of my strength, was imbued with the unyielding support of the one who bestowed it. Every misstep was met with gentle guidance, every stumble with renewed encouragement. His presence, a constant beacon in the midst of the storm, ensured that the mission bore fruit.

Maybe my journey seems impossible, a climb only for superheroes. But trust me, I'm more ordinary than you think. Just like you, I had doubts, fears, and days where the climb felt endless. But with a little bit of grace, a whole lot of hustle, and a heart full of hope, anyone can turn their "someday" into "today."

Driven by my own compelling life story, I lay bare its entirety within these pages. As a Nigerian woman born into a challenging childhood, I clawed my way to the pinnacle of success through sheer grit and the unwavering light of talent. Divine providence, the very foundation of my existence, has a way of sculpting us from the raw clay of circumstance, shaping lives towards a brighter destiny.

I hope my story isn't just about me; I hope it becomes a torch for you to light your own path. So go ahead, grab that dream like a shooting star, fuel it with your passion, and watch it soar. After all, the sky is not the limit – it's just the beginning!

Made in the USA
Middletown, DE
27 July 2024